Voice Training Through Acting and Movement

Voice Training Through Acting and Movement

An Integrated Approach

Chris Palmer

methuen | drama
LONDON • NEW YORK • OXFORD • NEW DELHI • SYDNEY

METHUEN DRAMA

Bloomsbury Publishing Plc, 50 Bedford Square, London, WC1B 3DP, UK
Bloomsbury Publishing Inc, 1359 Broadway, New York, NY 10018, USA
Bloomsbury Publishing Ireland, 29 Earlsfort Terrace, Dublin 2, D02 AY28, Ireland

BLOOMSBURY, METHUEN DRAMA and the Methuen Drama logo are
trademarks of Bloomsbury Publishing Plc

First published in Great Britain 2026

Copyright © Chris Palmer, 2026

Chris Palmer has asserted her right under the Copyright, Designs and
Patents Act, 1988, to be identified as Author of this work.

For legal purposes the Acknowledgements on pp. xxv–xxvii constitute an
extension of this copyright page.

Cover image: Mouth © AdobeStock

Online resources to accompany this book are available
at https://www.bloomsburyonlineresources.com/
voice-training-through-acting-and-movement. If you
experience any problems, please contact Bloomsbury
at: onlineresources@bloomsbury.com.

All rights reserved. No part of this publication may be: i) reproduced or
transmitted in any form, electronic or mechanical, including photocopying,
recording or by means of any information storage or retrieval system
without prior permission in writing from the publishers; or ii) used or
reproduced in any way for the training, development or operation of
artificial intelligence (AI) technologies, including generative AI
technologies. The rights holders expressly reserve this publication from
the text and data mining exception as per Article 4(3) of the Digital Single
Market Directive (EU) 2019/790.

Bloomsbury Publishing Plc does not have any control over, or
responsibility for, any third-party websites referred to or in this book.
All internet addresses given in this book were correct at the time of going
to press. The author and publisher regret any inconvenience caused if
addresses have changed or sites have ceased to exist, but can accept
no responsibility for any such changes.

A catalogue record for this book is available from the British Library.

Library of Congress Control Number: 2025943289.

ISBN: HB: 978-1-3503-8635-8
PB: 978-1-3503-8634-1
ePDF: 978-1-3503-8636-5
eBook: 978-1-3503-8637-2

Typeset by RefineCatch Limited, Bungay, Suffolk
Printed and bound in Great Britain

For product safety related questions contact
productsafety@bloomsbury.com.

To find out more about our authors and books visit www.bloomsbury.com
and sign up for our newsletters.

In honour of my mother Rita Mary Palmer,
your unwavering courage and loud voice still echoes through my heart.
It's time to sleep and rest those weary bones.

And in honour of my father Frank Charles Palmer,
you knew how to have a good time, all the time.

Contents

List of illustrations   x
List of videos   xi
Foreword: Neil Swain   xii
Preface for teachers   xv
Preface for students   xix
Videos   xxii
Acknowledgements   xxv

Introduction   1
     An overview   4
     My philosophy   6

1   Posture and Alignment Through Yin Yoga   9
     Introduction   9
     The spine and active rest   11
     Warm-up   14
     Posture   17
     Yin yoga (video)   21
     Cool-down – body scan and mindfulness script   32

2   Breath – Through Michael Chekhov, Inspired by Tai Chi   37
     Introduction   37
     Breath and distinctive styles of breathing   39
     Inspired tai chi and breath into sound   41

Breathing muscles and anatomy 44
Michael Chekhov through breath and imagination 54

3 Stamina – Inspired by Tadashi Suzuki 71

Introduction 71
Warm-up of toes, feet and legs 73
Squats 78
Tadashi Suzuki walks into sound and speech 83
Statues sitting and standing 86
Cool-down body scan 92

4 Pitch and Pace – 'Viewpoints' Inspired 95

Introduction 95
Warm-up the five senses 96
'Viewpoints' of space, shape, gesture, tempo and topography 99

5 Articulation Through Inspired Laban Efforts 121

Introduction 121
Body, senses, tongue, ears 122
Warm-up articulators 126
Consonants 127
Laban efforts of movement, breath, sound and text 137

6 Resonance – Meisner Inspired 145

Introduction 145
Warm-up resonance 146
Voice funnels 152
Repetition in resonance 155
Listening and responding 156
Calls and shouts 162

7 The Embodied Actor – Konstantin Stanislavski 165

Introduction 165
Prepare the body – warm-up 166

    Breath, sound and imagination   168
    Circles of attention and concentration   170
    Emotional recall   177
    Methods of physical action   178
    Body scan cool-down   180

Appendix 1: Sample curriculum   187
Appendix 2: Bibliography and resources   191
Index   193

Illustrations

1.1	The spine	11
1.2	Bowtie	29
1.3	Eagle arms	30
1.4	Thread the needle	31
2.1	The diaphragm: showing the falling and rising on inhalation and exhalation	45
2.2	The ribcage	46
2.3	Blowing up a balloon	49
2.4	Blowing up a beach ball	50
2.5	The vocal folds open	52
2.6	The vocal folds closed	52
3.1	Wind pose	75
3.2	Happy baby pose	76
3.3	Caterpillar pose	77
3.4	Squat pose Malasana	78
6.1	Suppress the alien	148
6.2	Stuck in a glass pyramid	151
6.3	Voice funnel	152
7.1	Circles of attention and concentration	171
7.2	The vagus nerve	182
7.3	The chakras	183

Videos

Chapter 1
Yin yoga poses with breath and sound.

Chapter 2
Inspired tai chi and Michael Chekhov with sound.

Chapter 3
Inspired Suzuki walks with breath and sound.
Standing and crouching statues with breath and sound.

Chapter 4
'Viewpoints' of shape and sound.

Chapter 5
Laban efforts with breath and sound.

Chapter 6
Meisner and resonance, oyster shell movement with breath and sound.

Chapter 7
Three circles of attention and concentration.

All videos are hosted on the companion website, available here: **https://www.bloomsburyonlineresources.com/voice-training-through-acting-and-movement**

Foreword by Neil Swain

Chris and I are united by two formative institutions: Rose Bruford College of Speech and Drama, as it was formerly known, and what is now known and deservedly so as The Royal Central School of Speech and Drama. Historically, both of these institutions were run by practitioners – not academics, accountants or businesspeople, but rather teachers who imparted craft and technique. Rose Bruford was a much-respected teacher of voice and movement, and the Central School had as its first principal the redoubtable Elsie Fogerty, and later the no less formidable Gwynneth Thurburn – fine voice teachers both. The fundamental importance of voice and speech in an actor's training was enshrined in the very names of both of these institutions.

After working in several UK drama schools, Guildford School of Acting being one, I was extremely fortunate in being invited to join the voice department at The Royal Shakespeare Company (RSC), which, as the only full-time department of its type in any theatre company in the world, was dedicated to working alongside and supporting both actors and directors alike. This was achieved for the life of the play, from first read through to rehearsals, then previews and the run as a whole, whether in one space, multiple auditoria or on tour. The RSC voice department owed its philosophy, success and indeed longevity to the tireless skill, passion and curiosity of the late great Cicely Berry, and to that of her Head of Voice, Andrew Wade. Cis very much believed in 'doing the work', and the importance of ongoing training. A company of actors with varying ages, backgrounds, experience and training were given the opportunity for continued work on voice, body, language and imagination. Through hearing, sensing and speaking the text, supported by the framework of solid technique (or as the Polish director Jerzy Grotowski would often liken it, the riverbank to the river), one can be open and vulnerable to the word – to be changed by the text as we speak it: 'God guard me from those thoughts men think in the mind alone; He that sings a lasting song Thinks in a marrow bone', *A Prayer Before Dying*, W. B. Yeats.

In recent years there has been a debate within some institutions that train actors, about the continued need for regular skills-based training, with some arguing that the professional demands of the modern actor no longer necessitates the need for a classical theatrical training. Some years ago, I was collaborating with an actor on a film. We were filming in Malta in the summer, and it was approaching forty degrees! His character had to deliver a long speech from a scaffold to a large attendant crowd. He was a very well-known and experienced classically trained Spanish actor and was working in English. He had to film the scene over several days with many different set ups. What got him through was technique. We worked as if we were tackling a piece of classical text, on phrasing, breath support, finding the length of the thoughts (how we breathe is how we think), on muscularity of speech and knowing when to save both his voice and performance. At the end of filming his scenes he said that it had reminded him of playing Shakespeare in the theatre. The modern actor needs solid technique, even more now than ever. Whether it be dealing with microphones in a live theatrical space; wrestling with a sometime convoluted or challenging script; the muscularity of speech and kinaesthetic awareness needed for seamless accent and dialect work; the understanding of and the ability to change voice quality in order to move from playing either a superhero to voicing an animated character or a video game; to effortlessly portray multiple characters whilst narrating an audio book; or to replicate as closely as possible the original delivery and performance in an Automated Dialogue Replacement (ADR) suite as part of post production.

Many years ago, a very well-known American sound mixer said to me that, 'Actors need to realise that a microphone can only amplify what it is given. It will never make a mumble any clearer!'. I have never forgotten that. So, just as a concert pianist practises for hours, or a ballet dancer repeats choreography or exercises at the barre, so with the aid of Chris's wonderfully clear exercises and her 'broad church' approach, the actor can continue to work on, hone and even challenge their technique. It is this continued work, rather than limiting the spontaneity of the actor as some modern acting gurus might have us believe, which actually provides us with a safety net, the riverbank to our creative river allowing it to flow with true freedom of expression.

Neil Swain's extensive career extends to: Voice Department at The Royal Shakespeare Company working alongside Cicely Berry, Andrew Wade, Lyn Darnley and John Barton, working on over thirty productions. After leaving the RSC, Neil has worked at The Royal National Theatre with Nicholas Hytner, The Royal Court, The Old and Young Vic Theatres, most of the UK regional repertory theatres, and many productions in the West End. He has had a busy few years working on Broadway with Michelle Williams in *Cabaret*. His work on television and film include *Rome*, *Hot Fuzz*, *An Education*, *Atonement*, *Macbeth*, *Cruella*, *Nolly* starring Helena Bonham Carter, and the multi-award-winning *The King's Speech*, *The Favourite* and *Poor Things*.

Preface for teachers

This workbook has been a long journey of discovery working in the actor training industry for many years. As a child actor I gained much knowledge through performing as a child singer and actor, but extraordinarily little understanding of the process of acting and the vocal and physical demands of the 'how to' until I went to Rose Bruford College of Speech and Drama. Understanding the philosophy of actor training meant I had to retrain my school of thought as a performer to deliver with authenticity.

For those teachers and facilitators that work within the context of a drama school, *conservatoire*, or performing arts school setting, you will gain a clearer understanding of voice training, by also navigating acting and movement methodologies. This book aims to interrogate the landscape and scope of voice, movement and acting pedagogies, applying methods from a national and international perspective, which underpin actor training for the twenty-first century. Adopting an integrated approach to voice teaching will allow the authenticity of the actors' voices to be heard, with skill, range and embodiment. Developing somatic awareness will help your students apply a range of choices from their bag of opportunities, developing embodied awareness and adapting to directorial styles, creating a flexible voice and body with a professional attitude required to work within an everchanging theatrical context.

As Head of Voice for over twenty years at Guildford School of Acting, University of Surrey, writing curricula to meet the ever-changing demands of the theatrical industry, whilst maintaining currency, efficacy and recognising the historical training of the past, in order to adapt and influence future voice training, has brought about what I believe to be a coherent and integrated method of delivery.

This workbook of *Voice Training Through Acting and Movement: An Integrated Approach*, has felt like I have been cultivating a garden, one that needs watering, weeding, feeding and allowing time to develop, and finally to blossom and bloom. Collaborating with actors is deeply personal, and therefore it has taken many years to develop this practice, whilst acknowledgeing the influence of other practitioners. As I continue to develop my own practice to support the learning of others, my journey is not yet finished but ever evolving. The primary aim of this workbook is to experience voice training in an integrated way, offering a wide range of voice training to empower and emancipate the actor, allowing the voice teaching to move from the silo of a single skill to the community of arts, which is multifaceted, inclusive and universal. I have explored at great length the intricacies and differences of acting and movement methodologies, and as the innovator of the groundbreaking MA in Teaching and Practice of Voice and Singing, I developed an integrated approach, which was realised in my first book *Voice and Speech for Musical Theatre*, published by Methuen Drama. I have now sought to create a parallel voice-training workbook that would accomplish the integration of voice into acting and movement skills. This is to support teachers, not to replace them. I am no specialist in any of the other skills, merely a lifelong student of them, and I seek to find the connections not the separations of our unique set of skills, offering differing ways to support an actor through their training.

The language of this workbook is designed to be simple and useful to both students and teachers, alongside those interested in directing, movement teachers, singing teachers and acting teachers. Whilst the book is addressed to the actor, there are tips for teachers in each chapter, and suggestions where you, the teacher, can demonstrate some of the exercises, giving you a greater degree of confidence in teaching some practical voice exercises whilst understanding the valuable training in movement and acting. There are also questions after each section for the student, in italics, designed to provoke and engage them to think critically about what each exercise has taught them, or to question what they may feel in terms of their breath or speech or resonance and how they perceive or meet each exercise. These are to be used as homework, in preparation for the coming class. The questions are prompts to further explore and deepen the journey through the exercises, and I have also included a curriculum for two semesters or three terms. There is also a companion website at: https://www.bloomsburyonlineresources.com/voice-training-through-acting-and-movement.

I advise students to keep a voice journal as part of their discovery, and a list of exercises that work for them, alongside how the work made them feel, and what is their daily take-away? This too can be a reflective journal of practice that you, the teacher, can use as basis for your students' understanding, and a starting point of discussion.

I also ask at the beginning of each year for students to record themselves and to keep the recording for reflection. It often astonishes them to listen back to the recording on how they sounded at the beginning of their voice journey after some time has elapsed (towards the last lesson of the term, semester or year), when you and they are able to reflect, without judgement. A passage of text at the end of each chapter is listed to support the work further, and this can be a wonderful way to explore your students' understanding of how far they have come through the work.

Through this book you will encounter some key principles in acting movement and voice. You will develop knowledge of human expression and integrate and interrogate voice training through other methodologies.

I hope you will find *Voice Training Through Acting and Movement: An Integrated Approach*, an exciting and diverse delivery of voice training, exploring potential, developing stamina and aiding confidence, whilst allowing authenticity and courage to develop your students' voices and yours too. As a teacher you will want to demonstrate the level and intensity with which you wish your students to engage, this will help harness the students' abilities (of course, always checking for any injuries, breathing issues, etc., in advance of any exercise), so I have given a list of learning outcomes which you may find useful.

Learning outcomes

The outcomes of this book are to:

- Explore and develop the foundations for a solid technical ability in relation to voice and speech through acting and movement.
- To expand your personal confidence in voice, speech, text and character work.
- To deepen and expand your knowledge of some well-known acting and movement practitioners.
- To enhance your understanding and support of your authentic speaking voice (social voice).
- To broaden and deepen your performance voice with stamina (performative voice).
- To secure the integration of acting skills in voice, movement and speech (integrated voice).
- To stimulate a desire for further development, either for personal enjoyment or future professional training (individual voice).
- To develop a vocal training approach to acting and movement that can work with a wide range of directors.

Preface for students

Welcome to *Voice Training Through Acting and Movement: An Integrated Approach*. You may be asking yourself, 'What does integration of voice mean? What does it mean to have voice and speech classes when I already know how to speak? How can I access my voice training through completely different methodologies in movement and acting?'. These are just some of the questions I suspect you may be thinking. Students can often understand why they need movement classes or acting classes, but voice classes might seem a bit baffling. You may think it is about shouting safely or using more volume or even accent work. It is so much more than that! My aim is to support you on your vocal journey of discovery whether performing in a small studio, a large outside space such as the Globe, or voice work for TV or film. It is also my aim to support your authentic voice, and although accents are a part of voice training, that is not all voice training is. This book is about supporting your voice healthfully, so that you may have a sustained and lengthy career in performing using your power and volume, your pitch range and resonance, through acting methods you may come across.

This workbook and set of short videos is designed to show you how to work on your voice individually, in pairs or in a group, and provide a daily practice that you can dip into and to support anything you wish to perform. Each exercise starts from the expectation that your current knowledge may be limited regarding the performative spoken voice. It then builds on that foundational knowledge and builds to more advanced fundamental voice work so that you may reach your vocal potential.

You may be thinking about applying to a drama school, *conservatoire* or performing arts programme or you may already be in a *conservatoire* that uses some of the acting and movement methodologies, in which case welcome to some interconnectedness. You may find that some of the exercises overlap an acting class or a movement session, and that has been a conscious decision, as it asks you to develop an understanding of the relationship between the other disciplines in actor training. They may also help explain some of the myths surrounding breath and stamina and breath support, core strength and its value in a voice class. This workbook will demystify those questions or conflicts and seek to create an understanding of them, rather than compromise one skill over another.

All the exercises are clearly laid out for you to explore, both in a class structure with your teacher, or on you own. You will further develop your vocal power, agility and flexibility, which will help you have a more efficient voice, be a more creative performer, and own your sound with authenticity. This will also secure a safe and healthy way to perform. To demonstrate the exercises, there are several short videos where students on a range of performance programmes at Guildford School of Acting work through the exercises that we have already done many times before. This will help you explore some of the exercises correctly and allow you time to move through the book, referring to sections repeatedly. Stop the video and go through the exercises until you feel more comfortable doing them. This will give you confidence. This book is aimed at you and your own learning.

I would always suggest keeping a journal of your voice practice, as this is an excellent way to reflect and record your own vocal development. Equally, I recommend recording your speaking voice at the beginning of this workbook. Do not put on a voice, just record something such as 'what you did at the weekend' then forget about the recording. Do not judge yourself at the beginning of your recording.

Leave the recording until you have completed all seven sections of the book, then come back to it, and hear yourself, hear the vocal changes that your voice has experienced through the exercises. I would suggest that you take about nine months to a year to complete this workbook, which allows time for you to complete all the exercises with rigour. You will see that there are questions in each section, chapter, by chapter to help guide you to what you might wish to write down. Each section will ask questions that are in italics, such as *'How does that feel?'* for you, the learner, to truly connect with the exercises and become autonomous learners.

I hope that *Voice Training Through Acting and Movement: An Integrated Approach* will bring you much success on your vocal journey towards becoming a professional actor.

Videos

This practical workbook is accompanied by a series of short videos of some of the exercises from each chapter where relevant. I have used some of the students at Guildford School of Acting (GSA) at MA and BA level on various programmes to demonstrate the practical application, which you can use and stop to recapture the work as often as you would like, to support a daily practice. The videos that accompany this book are a guide and will never take the place of a good voice teacher in the room but may allow the potential to support the workbook further.

The exercises are limited in terms of number and time, but I will suggest appropriate length of time for each exercise within this workbook. As a teacher, you might want to set some of the exercises as research and allow the students to develop a sense of autonomy within the work, or you may wish to use some of the exercises as a warm-up in which case the timings can be adjusted to suit the task you have set. It maybe that you wish to 'flip' the class for a session. A strategy where, as part of your students' homework, you set them the task of watching the exercises of the video as groundwork for you to develop further in your practice or lesson. This will help develop their sense of autonomy. Many of the exercises take much longer than what you will find on the video, as they are there as guidance only and designed as such to support the workbook and voice training.

If you are a student, you can use the videos as a guide to a daily practice. You will find this workbook uses your imagination, exploring imagery to clarify shapes, sounds, thoughts, feelings and nuances. Embodying the voice work asks you to explore the vocal landscape and interrogate expression as an actor. You will explore a range of voice-, body- and movement-based methodologies, connecting to the body through experiential anatomy (feel the work) and a vibrant truthful relationship with your imagination.

This workbook uses imagery that has worked for me and my students to encourage and support the creative imagination. Some of the names of the exercises have been suggested by students who collaborated on what each exercise should be called, but feel free to change the names that best suit you. The meditative aspects of the work might also encourage a positive mental attitude and understanding of the self to support the work and the voice.

Having trained as a yin yoga teacher, where I also encountered online learning and videos to support the aims of the Yoga programme, I found this invaluable and aided my learning, where I was able to go back and work through the exercises time and again. This is what I hope for you all.

Actor training asks us to develop the mind, body and spirit, asking questions of you, the actor, which was first suggested by Konstantin Stanislavski: 'who am I ?, what do I want?, where am I ?, when am I?, how do I get what I want?, and why do I want it?'. These questions are part of character work and actor training, but they also serve the voice, using imagery to focus the mind and engage the body, adopting imaginative games, exploring the possibility of the actor training as a creative flexible athlete, one that I have mentioned in my earlier book, *Voice and Speech for Musical Theatre*. Each video will remind you of the breath being present in the body, and mindfulness before starting any sequence.

A word about health and safety: If you have any injuries, you should make sure your tutor is aware, and they may offer you some safe alternatives. Links to the individual exercises are provided, including a link to all videos.

Acknowledgements

This book would not have been possible without the support and encouragement of many individuals. Primarily, I would like to express my deepest gratitude to my mentors and students alike, who have deepened my understanding of voice training. Their wisdom and insights have inspired much of the content within these pages, and their eagerness to learn new strategies with me have been the driving force behind this book.

Voice Training Through Acting and Movement: An Integrated Approach, has been a wonderful exploration covering many years of research and learning. Bringing together the interconnectedness of voice and some of the major practitioners who have influenced and or supported me on this journey, whether it is via face-to-face workshops, books, online training courses or colleagues, their ongoing support and guidance has allowed me to flourish. My book is a combination of all their work, so I do not stand alone on this journey. I would like to thank the staff at Guildford School of Acting. The leadership of Catherine McNamara who created a calm, measured environment, and allowed research and creativity across the school to flourish and to hold its own place within the University of Surrey. Pippa Treharne, the School manager, who manages to make sure all events related to this book and my previous book *Voice and Speech for Musical Theatre* run smoothly. I would like to thank Sarah Sage, Theatre Technical Manager, and her staff who make sure all stage-managed events and supporting marketing work seamlessly. I would also like to thank Toby Pope, administrator, who helped with all things technical. I would like to thank Bronwyn McPhee for her inspirational artwork for this book, which sought to recognise my thoughts as ideas into an artistic reality.

I would also like to thank Niall Bailey, a friend, colleague and inspiration who has supported the use of the integrated voice through the acting and movement methodologies on his programme BA Actor Musicians; Stewart Nicholls, who has allowed me to thrive as an acting coach, and to put acting at the heart of musical theatre, allowing the integration of acting and voice training to work in a comprehensive way; and Nicholas Scrivens, who recognises that the voice teacher is also the director, who read and offered comments on chapters, and continues to support voice training as an integrated skill on the MA Musical Theatre programme.

Thanks to the wonderful teams on the BA and MA Acting Programmes. To Anna Tringham who provided much inspiration and workshops in the Laban Efforts; Dr Gerald 'jay' Paul Skelton, for his time and commitment to the 'Viewpoints' and inspirational workshops and my many questions; and Grainne Byrne for many chats about Michael Chekhov.

My thanks must go to student Louie Wanless who supplied some names of exercises and those students who gave freely their photos and drawings of their vision of each exercise, with thanks to Paloma Siblik and to students Leona Vaughn, Alexander Maliepaard, Josh Betesh, Ruth Douglas, Alexandra Evie, Bronwyn McPhee, Ry Granger, Mia Pocock, Parker Goldby, Elise Willhoft, Emilie Laurent, all who participated in the video and gave their time freely.

I would like to extend my thanks to the wonderful voice team at Guildford School of Acting: Barbara Ward, Jenny Tullet and Adam Wallis who read drafts of my chapters and whose passion for voice training both historical and current gave me a new drive and passion to continue to contribute to the field of voice training. Their insights into each chapter helped clarify my thoughts further.

To all the vocal artists and voice enthusiasts who continue to explore and push the boundaries of what the human voice can achieve, this book is dedicated to you. Your passion and dedication are what make this field continue to be exciting and dynamic. Heartfelt thanks to my partner Chris who looked after the house and cat while I rambled incessantly and listened whilst 'pretending' to be interested in the workings of each methodology through the voice, over dinner each night. To the music of Nirvana where Kurt Cobain still reigns supreme.

Special thanks must go to Beth Holton for taking photos in a voice class at the last minute and the students that took part: Paul Stevens, Edith Sedgwick, Joshua Ogier, Isabella Letterese, Keiran Powell, Oscar Vaughan, Helen Bellinger, Archie Agnew and Clementine Wright.

Finally, thanks must go to Anna Brewer, Dr Aanchal Vij, Merv Honeywood at RefineCatch Limited, Simon Proctor and David Carey, all who helped make this journey much easier for me.

Introduction

For many years I have practiced meditation, yoga and tai chi, and explored the physiological and psychological aspects of this work, which I bring into my voice teaching. Actors often face unique challenges from balancing intense work schedules with job insecurities and navigating the physical and vocal demands of the entertainment industry in all its forms, from working or auditioning one day for a voice-over, to the next day working with green screen and then off to perform in a show. The practices of tai chi, yoga and meditation cultivates mindfulness and can be transformative for an actor's well being.

When researching this book, I discovered many practitioners had a similar interest. For example, most of the acting and movement pioneers I have been researching had some form of training in meditation and yoga. Mary Overlie trained as a transcendental meditation teacher in 1968; Rudolph Laban explored meditation and the works of Carl Jung and his philosophies of psychological types; Konstantin Stanislavski explored the embodied actor through yoga, and later through self-awareness and mindful meditation; Tadashi Suzuki developed a method of teaching through the culture of the body and created a philosophy of mindfulness to become comfortable in body through rigour and stillness and further explored the relationship between human and animal; Sanford Meisner delved into the world of mindfulness and meditation, body work and imagination; and Michael Chekhov used meditation and yoga. All of the above searched for the authentic way to teach actors, to explore the imagination, to observe, to truly listen and, finally, to understand the integration of voice and body and our place in the world around us.

In my own actor training as a professional actor and singer, I was often looking for connections between voice training, acting methodologies and movement classes. Some skills classes developed a sense of the interconnectedness and the psychology of acting, but within other skills classes I, personally, struggled to grasp the reasons for the class, or an exercise, or even the purpose of an entire project. This was my own inability to critically reflect on the work, and I lacked at times an understanding of integration, through the skills, and what was being offered by some of the classes, where I imagined the classes were working independently of each other, hoping that us, the students, would make those connections. I am aware as a learner, that I need the signposting to be more obvious than my fellow actors, one who needs a clear instruction of what the skill is and how I can apply the work into other performing areas, in order to be empowered by the work.

Increasingly, actor training is becoming dual focused in delivery, to be multifaceted and inclusive, as evidenced in various books on offer, with acting and movement as an integrated subject, or voice and acting, or voice and singing, etc. This shows there is a need to exemplify the connectedness and the integration of skills, so that the actor is truly embodied in the work, and where the signposting is clearer.

I hope this book offers you an increased awareness of the integrated multiskilled performer, which can be transformative, much like what is often proposed in the musical theatre training of the 'triple threat performer'. I also hope that by contributing to the existing and valued work in voice, acting, movement methodologies and practices, that actor training is considered a triple or quadruple threat too.

During the pandemic, this work became more reinforced, when I found myself one day considering how I could support students at home more efficiently. Reflecting on my own actor training, I began to rediscover my own skills, such as the love of

Laban Efforts, the walks and statues of Suzuki, the directions and gestures of Michael Chekhov and the embodied work of Stanislavski. Through the online and hybrid delivery grew for me a distinctive style of teaching voice for actors, one where I, the voice tutor, was also the movement tutor and the acting coach. I suppose I took the opportunity of the pandemic to work harder to bring about elements of the training together. This created an integration of voice skills that has developed further and deeper into a vocal practice, now years on from those times where I was able to weave the delivery of voice skills training, to truly sit as an integrated acting fundamental. My own continuing development focused on rediscovering an interconnectedness to voice training and Laban Efforts; voice training and Mary Overlie's and Anne Bogart's 'Viewpoints'; voice training and Michael Chekhov's acting techniques; voice training in relation to the acting methods of Sandford Meisner techniques especially, but not exclusively, the use of repetitive work and listening skills; and of course the relationship of voice training and Stanislavski.

Teaching voice under these conditions inspired me to find new ways to create a context-driven curriculum and connect with other classes being taught, and those not taught. I was able to embrace those other elements of actor training in its current form, not just in the UK but internationally. This was a significant shift for me as a voice tutor to become an integrated voice tutor, one that directs, teaches acting, and understands elements of movement, tying the skill strands together.

This workbook is suitable for those with an interest in voice, acting and movement methodologies, and those who wish to pursue a career in the arts, as an actor, director, movement teacher, voice teacher or facilitator. You might be working through speech exams, you may be a voice and speech teacher, or a teacher of acting through song. Welcome.

You will find listed a voice curriculum for a twenty-week programme of three terms, or the two-semester approach designed to support your practice further. There are many wonderful publications and workbooks on each of the various disciplines and skills, sometimes there are books offering a combination of two skills; however, there is none that I am aware of that combines voice training with multiple acting and movement skills, giving a broad spectrum of specific exercises and a springboard to understanding the actor trainer in the twenty-first century.

An overview

This book is divided into seven chapters, each with subheadings, relating to voice training in drama schools, *conservatoires* and other performing arts institutes and further education schools at B-tec level, A level and beyond, and providing a bonding to the interconnectedness of voice training, acting and movement skills. Each chapter will provide further reading to supplement your learning, including suggested texts. There are tips for teachers that explore further suggestions of exercises and a sample curriculum for a framework of three terms or alternatively for two-semester frameworks. The timings of each 'lesson' allow for a 1 hour 45 minute lesson to 2 hours. I have aligned the voice training with a curriculum based on the actor training of a *conservatoire* to compliment the acting and movement skills and refer to them to preserve the interconnectedness and interdisciplinary nature of the work and this book. There is a specific warm-up designed as an introduction to the methodology in each chapter and serves to heighten and preserve the awareness of each practitioner through that warm-up and develop a greater degree of pedagogic practice. There is a body scan, meditation, or cool-down linked to each practitioner as a cool-down. Each chapter starts with some suggestions of dictionary references to the overall aim of the chapter.

Chapter 1: 'Posture and Alignment Through Yin Yoga', focuses on good alignment for voice and speech, with particular reference to the spine, inspired by yin yoga and the elements of 'being present' drawing upon the mind and the body through embodiment. **Chapter 2:** 'Breath – Through Michael Chekhov and Inspired by Tai Chi', focuses on breath, movements of inspired tai chi and Michael Chekhov's directions and psychological gestures. **Chapter 3:** 'Stamina – Inspired by Tadashi Suzuki', focuses on extended breath and stamina, building the voice through leg and feet movements, range and expression. **Chapter 4:** 'Pitch and Pace – "Viewpoints" inspired', explores the voice training through Mary Overlie's and Anne Bogart's 'Viewpoints' of space, time and tempo building pitch through the work. **Chapter 5:** 'Articulation Through Inspired Laban Efforts', focuses on articulation, consonants and vocal improvisation and expression. **Chapter 6:** 'Resonance – Meisner Inspired', aims to harness resonance through voice funnels, exploring listening, repetition, power and volume through shouts, calls and safe screams. **Chapter 7:** 'The Embodied Actor Konstantin Stanislavski', aims to broaden and increase the vocal scope of choices through the work of Stanislavski, exploring circles of attention and concentration, imagination, emotional recall and psycho-physical acting.

Each chapter is structured to offer an element of vocal training that supports and clarifies each practitioner through body work, breath, resonance, pitch and articulation and to build upon the previous chapter with subheadings that follow a simple through line of 'Feel the work' followed by 'Understand the work' and finally 'Practice the work'.

There are 'Tips for teachers', with a thirty week curriculum, followed by suggested texts and further reading. The first section, 'Feel the work' is as it suggests, working through an exercise to explore 'what you feel'. The section titled 'Understand the work' explains what you have just explored and the discoveries you have made and what it is and why do it, and gives a deeper insight into the practitioners, with information to lead you to supporting evidence in further reading. Finally, the 'Practise the work' section capitalises on the ability to do the work alone and have autonomy as a learner and explore further.

My philosophy

I start each exercise by working through the body, then allowing a release of breath, then a sound, then a word, then finally the text. This sequence has allowed me to establish the principles that body, then breath, allows for vocal delivery to be free. Every exercise, every moment, is about making discoveries. This workbook aims to provide a link between the training of acting, the training of movement and the training of voice. The exercises I share with you work for me as a director, voice teacher, acting tutor, yin yoga teacher and tai chi practitioner, and some that do not.

Your journey is your journey, not my journey, and the way we learn is unique to us. So, look at how you learn and work through the book in a way that best suits you. You may find that you want to delve into various exercises in chapters as the moment takes you, and that is fine. You may find that a particular chapter or exercise connects with what you are discovering or working on right now in your acting or movement classes, so allow yourself the possibilities of supporting that work further.

I have put the chapters into a format that works for how I teach, going through them methodically. You may have a better approach than this and you can write your own curriculum based on what you read here; you could take an exercise from each chapter and create your own unique class. As mentioned, this workbook is about finding patterns and making connections.

There are many studies on how feedback and assessment work. Having been a student for many years, I noticed I was unable to hear the feedback the way the tutor intended it, partly because I was nervous, or desperate to hear that I was 'good' and did not want to hear any critical feedback. As a teacher I found my direct approach did not always work for everyone. So, a few years ago I created a study buddy system to support my students. This, firstly, involves a Student (A) to give feedback couched in terms such as 'what strengths I have gained, and what I need to strengthen further', which is presented to myself and the rest of the class. Then I give my feedback to Student (A) which involves two students listening to the feedback. One person (the buddy) or Student (B) writes down what the tutor (me) has said, whilst the person receiving the feedback, Student (A), is listening; they do not have to write down anything, just listen. Some use recording devices, but I personally prefer to allow the students to flick through their journals, seeing multiple feedback from myself via a third person, Student (B), writing the feedback in the student's journal. This has been a positive experience for both students and me, feeling they are heard about their learning processes and gives opportunity for myself to concur with the student, as this self-reflection is an acknowledgement and collaboration of what they have understood and what to do next.

This workbook aims to find connections between voice through integration, enjoying the process of learning, listening, problem solving and enjoying taking risks.

Further reading and suggested texts

Education is the most powerful weapon which you can use to change the world. *NELSON MANDELA*

The power of the word, spoken, written, or read, has the ability to shape education, change lives and create a movement or to disrupt the status quo. Having researched the books on the further reading listed in each chapter, I am only supported by their work. Each chapter sets out a list of suggested texts that are linked to the subject matter of that chapter. The reading list after each chapter helps solidify my own learning and shape where you can continue to delve into the wonderful work of other practitioners, writers, movements specialists, acting teachers and so on.

1 Posture and Alignment Through Yin Yoga

> The beauty of the trees, the softness of the air, the fragrance of the grass speaks to me. *INSPIRED BY AN INDIGNENOUS AMERICAN SAYING*

Standing meaning:

1. Stand to attention.
2. Left standing.
3. Stand alone.
4. Stand your ground.

Introduction

In this first chapter we will explore how your posture, alignment and an investigation of your spine can be developed through the principles of yin yoga. The reason I established yin yoga in my voice teaching practice many years ago was to function as a counterbalance to any high-energy movement work associated with actor training, and adopt the coolness of the yin energy to the heated yang-like energy of other body work such as the Suzuki Technique and Laban Efforts explored in later chapters. I like to start any daily voice practice by working through the spine. The spine or backbone has so many connotations attached to it. There is the literal meaning of the backbone being a series of vertebrae, extending from the skull to the coccyx. But it can also mean a series of common negative synonyms such as spineless, no backbone, being weak or cowardly, lacking courage or determination. Interestingly, the *Oxford Dictionary* suggests with reference 'to stand upright', that the common analogies are, conscientious, honest, courageous, to stand one's ground, and being grounded.

Your posture or alignment can suggest an attitude, a pose, or have a standpoint. To walk and stand upright as humans with maximum efficiency, we evolved through millions of years of evolution, and this is known as 'the dynamic posture'. Static posture is how you hold yourself when you are not moving. Activating the spine through yin yoga will support any daily vocal practice, reminding us of the human journey of evolution, and therefore is an effective way to start any voice work by creating a mindful understanding of the neutral posture, sitting, standing and the relationship to the spine.

What do we mean by the term 'a neutral posture' or good posture and alignment? Often when we hear this term, we are likely to stiffen and straighten up. The opposite of what you would want from a performer. As a short person of stature myself, I am aware that in the past I have thrust my neck forward to appear taller. In my actor training, learning about the Alexander Technique to support the connection to the spine in relation to movement and voice was so useful for me, and now I always check in with my neutral posture daily. A neutral posture is the position of the body that places the least stress on the musculoskeletal system while still allowing for maximum control and strength, therefore mindful of standing, sitting, breathing and resting to recognise and acknowledge habits.

The Alexander Technique is a wonderful exploration of understanding the 'neutral spine' and helps the efficiency of voice and speech further. Whilst we are all born physically different, as actors we want to gain maximum efficiency from our body and breath to serve our performative voice. So, understanding how our body works begins with the basics of good posture to secure optimum breath, and can be supported through mindful noticing. Mindful awareness is key to good optimum posture and being aware in action will give you choices to act and react. There are many mind–body disciplines such as meditation and yoga, and the aim is to explore developing mindfulness in posture.

Exploring our habitual standing and sitting poses, we can explore a greater degree of sound and movement, which is healthy, sustainable and achieves a greater degree of choice for you as an actor.

The spine and active rest

Feel the work

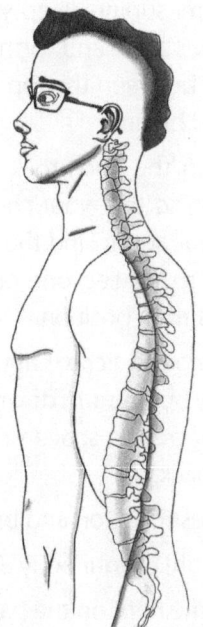

Figure 1.1 The spine.

Exercise 1: Semi-supine and active rest

Lie on your back on the floor, with your legs long and arms down by your side (supine).

Allow your feet to relax, your palms to face upwards, and close your eyes.

Take a moment to feel your body supported by the floor. Feel the air on the front and sides of the body. Allow yourself to sink into the floor, feeling supported as you relax the back of your body.

Stay here for 1 minute, inhaling and exhaling, allowing active rest to wash over you.

This is a classic corpse pose, also known as shavasana in yoga. It helps rejuvenate the mind and body.

Now bend your legs with your feet flat on the floor (semi-supine).

Now that you are in semi-supine, keep your buttocks on the floor, and rock your pelvis back and forth to find the midway point in the movement, between the top of the pelvis and the tailbone. Settle there and breathe.

Next, keep your head on the floor, rock your head back and forth, from chin to chest, so that your chin rises to the ceiling and then forwards to your chest. Find the midway point, settle there, and breathe. You may need one or more books to rest under your head for optimum position.

Now raise one arm up into the air so that the shoulder peels off the floor, and then gently put the arm down by your side. Repeat with the other arm. This creates space under the armpits and further flattens out the back.

Now settle in an active rest position and breathe.

Let the floor take the weight of your body. Stay here for 1 minute.

Notice the sensation of the floor on the back of your head, your back, your buttocks, your legs, your feet, and your spine against the floor, and feel your front body open.

Exercise 2: Standing and noticing

Now come into standing position.

Next, stand how you might normally stand and notice your posture. Now walk around the space as you normally would.

> *What part of the body do you lead from? Your chest? Your knees? Your head?*
>
> *What is your rhythm and pace?*
>
> *Do you walk fast or slow?*
>
> *Do you take long strides or short strides?*
>
> *Do you walk on the balls of your feet, on your heels, or on toes?*

Notice this about yourself.

Now stand with your feet parallel and the weight evenly distributed between big toe, little toe and heel of the foot. Think of a tripod at the bottom of your foot.

Now sway from side to side to feel the energy, in your feet, legs, hips and back.

Next rock your weight forward and back, rocking from heel to toe. Feel the balance of weight between heel and toe. Allow your shoulders to relax down, towards your hips and feet. Imagine your neck lengthening, feel your head balance upwards, your back lengthen and widen, your head moving with ease.

Now nod your head, yes and no. Your knees and hips joints and ankle joints are well balanced. Your feet are softening into the ground.

Now stand with feet hip distanced apart, with your knees feeling soft, as you lengthen in the spine, widening across the chest, arms and shoulders, your head gently balanced on top as if you were still lying on the floor. Remember the feeling of lying on the floor. You should feel grounded.

Repeat the following phrases whilst in this neutral position.

'My spine lengthens'.

'My rib cage widens'.

'My legs are ready for action'.

'I am aware of the space up above and the space below'.

'I am aware of the space to my left and to my right'.

'I am aware of the space behind me and in front of me'.

Tips for teachers
It is always good to check in with your students regarding any injuries, or where some adjustments might need to be made to support them. Also, this check in provides the opportunity to allow them time to reflect on their voice and bodies,

Warm-up

Before we start the warm-up ensure that you have repeated the standing and noticing exercise. Try to explore every exercise with mindfulness and conscious effort. Otherwise, it can seem perfunctory rather than a conscious effort of daily practice.

Exercise 3: Warm-up

Stand in neutral pose keeping your feet flat on the floor, reminding yourself of the weight distribution or the tripod. Stretch your arms above your head, reaching for your imaginary goal.

Stretch your fingertips, hands and shoulders in an upward motion. Now release the shoulders downwards, then release the wrists, the elbows and the arms. Release a sigh, or an /f/ sound.

Next, stretch your arms up again, only this time reach onto your toes. Then drop the feet, the shoulders, the arms and hands. Release a sigh, or an /f/ sound.

Next, stretch your arms once again and imagine you are a puppet, and on each joint strings are attached: from the wrists, the elbows, the shoulders, the chin to the chest. Then flop forwards and hang there, so that you are hanging forward in dangling pose. Release a sigh, or an /f/ sound.

Now very slowly come up to standing tall, vertebra by vertebra, and stretch up again letting out a sigh, or an /f/ sound.

Repeat the stretch to the flop several times to really access the spine, this time release the /f/ sound. Stay there in the flop for 30 seconds and feel the spine release vertebra by vertebra. (I like to think of my spine like a long bicycle chain.)

Slowly make your way up to fully upright and feel the sensation of length and height in your upper body.

Now raise your right arm up and reach over to the left side and feel the ribcage on the right.

Now pat the exposed ribcage with your left hand. Release on an /ah/.

Now repeat on the opposite side.

Exercise 4: Circles and wraps

Keeping your head in a neutral position, let your nose take a journey of circles to release the neck. Circle the nose creating small circles from your left shoulder to your right shoulder. Then repeat in the opposite way, keeping your eyes open and notice what you see as your head slowly moves round and round.

Taking your head back to neutral, drop the chin to the chest and feel the weight of the head as your chin rests on your chest. Notice the release or acknowledgement of tension in the back of your neck, then slowly bring your head back up to a neutral position and imagine your head feels as if it is bobbing on top of your spine.

Once again drop the chin to the chest and bring your nose towards your left armpit and count to ten. You may feel a release of tension in the opposite strap muscle.

Now bring your nose towards your right armpit and count to ten. Once again you may feel a release of tension in your opposite strap muscle.

Now wrap your arms around your body and hug yourself, then slowly bend forward with your legs bent, releasing forwards and downwards. Stay there for the count of ten.

Slowly come up and release your arms.

Now change the position of your arms and repeat the hug.

Place your hands on your hips, and imagine your knees feel soft. Circle the hips slowly ten times in one direction, repeating the word 'no'. Each time try and say the word 'no' differently, allowing the circles to get bigger. Now try with other words of your choice.

Now repeat the same exercise in the opposite direction allowing the circles to become smaller and repeat the word 'yes' each time. Make the word sound different each time you make a circle.

Now try a different word of your choice.

Tips for teachers

Your students could take turns in the daily joint rotation with their own words. Here are a few examples you may wish to use: happy and sad, good and evil, fish and chips, sausage and mash.

Practice the work

Continue with the knees soft, cup the knees with your hands and circle the knees slowly one way (clockwise) ten times in one direction followed by ten times in the opposite direction.

Finally, circle your feet to warm up the ankles slowly, clockwise ten times. Repeat in the opposite direction, then repeat with the other foot/ankle.

Now execute a quick body scan from toes up to the head and give yourself a mental tick as you check off each area. Notice how you feel in your mind.

Now stand with your feet parallel, the knees should feel soft but active, the feet active without tension. The weight ratio should feel equal between the front of the foot and the back of the foot. Once again think of a tripod.

Lengthen in your spine, and imagine every part of your spine from the coccyx or tailbone upwards towards the sacrum, then upwards towards the lumbar, then upwards towards your thoracic spine, then further upwards towards the neck and lengthen the vertebrae or cervical spine, upwards towards the head. Now imagine your head is floating high above your body like a balloon or a drone that is attached to the neck, notice what this does for your posture.

Your shoulders should be relaxed in a downward motion, your arms relaxed by your side. The weight should feel equal between the front of the foot and the back of the foot. You can sway back and forth until you feel you are in your centre. You are now standing in neutral posture, ready and awake.

Standing is a constant rebalancing act; we are not static or statues.

Posture

Understand the work: Alexander Technique

We have just worked on the very beginnings of the seminal work of the Alexander Technique. F. M. Alexander was an Australian actor in the 1890s who found he was losing his voice in performance. Observing himself and others he began a lifelong career in evaluation of his physical posture in performance and in everyday life. He was aware of his habitual posture and the damaging effects on his voice and body. He chose to spend the rest of his life dedicated to the proficiency in posture and alignment for efficiency, vocal health, and optimum use of standing, sitting, speaking and shouting. Many performing arts schools and *conservatoires* have incorporated his technique into either voice work or movement work to establish a healthy stance for the actor. Understanding your habitual posture plays a key role in how to practice and adopt the character work of others.

Practice the work: Neutral posture
Exercise 5: Balance and neutral posture

Stand with your feet hip distance apart, or if you are unsure, place your fist between your knees, this will give you a good guideline. Your knees should feel relaxed and soft. Your toes should feel open and separated, meaning your feet are alive and engaged. You can separate each toe with your fingers to fully notice the space between them. Remind yourself of the tripod and the ratio between big toe little toe, and heel of the foot.

Your torso should feel wide and long. Imagine every vertebra having space of its own all the way up to your neck where your head gentle bobs. Allow your head to nod 'yes' and 'no' a few times.

Allow the arms to hang gently from the shoulders, with elbows and wrist and hands open and relaxed.

Allow yourself to lean forwards and notice if your toes over-grip to keep yourself from falling forward.

Next allow yourself to lean backwards and notice if the back of your legs over-engage to stop yourself from falling backwards.

Sway back and forth a few times to find the middle ground. Lean slightly forwards so that 60 per cent of your weight is at the front of your body and 40 per cent is at the back of your body, this allows for you to be ready and engaged. Notice if this feels out of kilter or odd.

Now try 50 per cent on the front of the foot and 50 per cent at the back of the foot. This is known as neutral posture, where the position of the body is at ease for a prolonged period, and is an efficient way of walking, sitting and standing. Too much contraction either inward or outward makes the body rigid and inflexible, when as an actor your body needs to be dynamic and springy so that it can move and breathe freely. To escape rigidity and make choices we need to make informed choices with control and ease, so that performances are free, organic and exciting.

Now stand in the neutral pose and notice how your body and mind feel.

Try playing with the weight ratio and notice how you feel, emotionally, physically, psychologically. Observe your posture when you begin to play characters of different ages and temperaments. This will really support character development by understanding posture, what it might feel like to lose some flexibility as ageing affects the posture, or an illness or tension.

Exercise 6: Improvising around posture

Explore yourself slumped over in a relaxed way; a cool dude, or a lazy way of standing so that you notice if your legs come together or move far apart. Observe how it makes you feel psychologically, emotionally, as well as physically, and notice how it makes you breathe. *How does it affect your thinking?*

Next try walking around in this stance for a while. Notice what thoughts come into your head. You may notice your mind may race fast or be slow. Take some time in this posture and enjoy it. Notice if it affects the breath or sound.

Next move back into the neutral pose and notice how different this is from the 'cool dude' one. Notice as you walk around whether your thoughts and feelings are affected, or your breath for example. Notice if your breath feels deep or shallow.

Now move to a pose that is rigid and stiff. Perhaps consider a soldier as a choice. Notice your thoughts and feelings and breathing associated with this pose. Notice what emotions you are experiencing.

Now try walking and talking in each of the poses and notice how it affects the rate or speed of speech depending on which pose you are in. Make notes on your breath, your feelings, your attitude, your speed at which you speak. This would be a good place to journal your thoughts and the effects of each walking and standing pose. They may offer some character choices for you.

Now move back to the neutral pose.

Practice the work: Stretch and release

Exercise 7: Puppet

Take a wide stance with legs apart.

Stretch your arms high above your head and open your mouth wide and let out a yawn or a sigh allowing a few seconds in this expansive stance. Now let your arms drop to the side.

Next stretch your arms wide again allowing your fingers to expand too – open your mouth wide and let out a yawn or a sigh, allowing a few seconds in this state. Then let your arms drop to the side.

Now stretch again and feel your whole body expand down to your hips and legs – open your mouth wide and let out a yawn or a sigh or sound, and let your arms drop to the sides.

Now stretch again and this time let your wrists drop with a release of breath, then your elbows, then your shoulders, then your head, then flop forward from the waist down so that your hands are brushing the floor (puppet).

Slowly uncurl your spine and raise yourself up vertebra by vertebra so that your spine becomes stacked, leaving your chin on your chest.

Raise your chin from your chest as you raise your head up and slowly allow the arms to raise high above your head again.

Repeat this entire sequence a few times to feel the expanse in your body and the difference in energy as you release body parts a little at a time.

Raise the shoulders up to the ears and then release on a sigh, and repeat three times.

Tips for teachers

You could ask your students to work in pairs so that they are able to see their habitual pose and then help their partners engage with the neutral posture further. Understanding one's own habitual pose (like my own neck thrust) allows for your students or yourself some reflection, as we begin to understand how to gain the most from neutral posture. This allows for more choices as an actor and a greater degree of fluidity when understanding bodies in space. Beginning each session with a body scan to start each session allows your students to see how they use their bodies efficiently and can support a greater degree of breath support and energy. Also, this can support a feeling of confidence.

Yin yoga

Feel the work: Yin yoga poses (on video)

Exercise 8: Deer pose

Start by sitting on the floor in a butterfly pose, with your feet sole to sole, and swing one leg behind your body, leaving the remaining knee in a bent position. You will see that your legs look like the antlers of a deer. The front of the body is open. Next take your hands behind you and rest them on the floor. Now lean backwards with your head in neutral. Stay here for 2 minutes. Now breathe freely into the ribs, belly and back. This pose increases hip flexibility, improves works on your hips and lower back and can help with digestion.

On inhalation feel your ribs expand and belly expand, and on each exhalation feel a release as your body succumbs to gravity and into the pose.

Repeat on the opposite side.

Exercise 9: Low-flying dragon pose

On all fours or tabletop position, step the left leg out between your hands making sure the left knee is aligned with the ankle, dropping your right knee towards the floor. Extend a gentle stretch into the groin. Stay here for around 2 minutes. Repeat on the other side. Now breathe freely into the ribs, belly and back. Inhale and exhale using steady breaths.

On inhalation feel your ribs and belly expand and a release in the hips and groin, and on each exhalation feel a release as your body succumbs to gravity and into the pose.

This pose increases hip mobility, creating length in your lower back and supports any issues around sciatica.

Repeat on the other side.

Exercise 10: Spinal twist pose

Lying on your back bring the arms out to the sides, bend your legs so that you are in semi-supine and take both legs over the right side. The shoulder on the opposite side (left side) will want to come off the floor so the aim is to relax this shoulder down to the floor. This may mean your legs open, and so by putting a cushion between your legs will, allow gravity to release the legs slowly to a closed position. Now breathe freely into the ribs, belly and back.

On inhalation feel your ribs and belly expand, feel a release in the lower back and mid back. On each exhalation feel a release as your body succumbs to gravity and into the pose. Stay here for 4 minutes.

This pose is also known as an axial rotation which helps lubricate the spine and increases a range of motion, supports digestion through some compression of the internal organs and supports the lower back. Now breathe freely into the ribs, belly and back.

Repeat on the other side.

Exercise 11: Supported fish pose

This is a reclining back bend pose. Using a cushion, block or bolster, which should be in the upper middle part of the back, lie on your back, feeling the open sensation to the front of the body as you relax back with your head back, your throat can be open and supported. You can choose to bend the legs or keep them stretched out in front, alternatively you could move your legs into butterfly pose. Spend up to 4 minutes in this pose.

On inhalation feel your back, ribs and belly expand, feel a release in the upper back and on each exhalation feel a release as your body succumbs to gravity and into the pose.

This pose invites you to mindfully stretch the muscles around the ribcage as it opens the neck, chest and intercostal muscles. This is an energising pose. Now breathe freely into the ribs, belly and back, connecting with the front of the body.

Exercise 12: Sphinx pose

Lie on your front body and line up your elbows with your shoulders and your forearms flat out in front of you. Imagine you look like a cactus.

Make your legs long and slightly wider apart to allow the thighs to support your lower back and reduce any pinching in your lower back. This will also prevent you from tightening your buttocks. You want to be relaxed and open.

Next raise your upper body, keeping the arms bent so that you look like the sphinx of Egypt. Now breathe into the belly and feel yourself carve a bowl in the floor with your stomach. Stay here for around 4 minutes in total.

On inhalation feel your belly expand into the floor, and a release in the buttocks and openness of the throat, and on each exhalation feel a release as your body succumbs to gravity and into the pose.

This pose opens the lungs, chest and shoulders and raises your energy levels. Now breathe freely into the ribs, belly and back. As you breathe into the belly and feel a bowl in the floor you may find your hips rock back and forth.

Exercise 13: Wide-legged child's pose

Get into a position on your knees, with your legs wide and your big toes touching, allow the weight of the body to rest back as much as you can on your feet. Extend the arms out in front with head rested on the floor. Allow up to 4 minutes in this pose, releasing the belly. Now breathe freely into the ribs, belly and back.

On inhalation feel your belly and ribs expand, a release in the hips and groin and on each exhalation feel a release as your body succumbs to gravity and into the pose.

This pose gently stretches the spine and the ankles. It massages the organs for digestion through compression.

Exercise 14: Dangling to standing pose

From the child's pose, tuck your toes under and bring yourself back onto your feet, and push your body onto your feet. Fold forwards, with your knees bent, allowing your spine to curl round. To enhance this further cross your arms or cup your hands to your elbows. Spend up to 5 minutes in total and breathe. Slowly uncurl the spine vertebra by vertebra.

On inhalation feel your ribs expand and a release in the spine. On each exhalation feel a release as your body succumbs to gravity and into the pose.

This is the only standing pose in yin yoga and it decompresses the spine, massages the organs for digestion and increases flexibility in the hamstrings. Now breathe freely into the ribs, belly and back.

Understand the work: Yin yoga

Yin yoga is vastly different from other types of yoga, stretching in a gentle and mindful way, allowing gravity to support the time (long hold), to passively stretch and target the focus of sensation, to release for a particular area. It is regarded as the cool feminine quality energy of yoga. Yin yoga is based on the principles of find your edge, maintain the hold and be mindful to be still, so that your body relaxes into a pose for quite a long time, from between 2 and 8 minutes, and letting gravity take the weight of your body. These poses are held for some time to release connective tissue, the fascia and tissue that surrounds joints, so that eventually you have more freedom to move with choice. You may feel more opening in one side, of the body over another side which is quite normal. You may also feel emotional as your body releases tension that you may not have even been aware of. Notice this and practice often. Yin yoga derives from two distinct lines of yoga practices. The Chinese Taoist philosophy and the Indian hatha yoga practices of mindful, calm and passive release. I use this in my teaching of voice as the body becomes freer the breath becomes freer, and the sound of voice becomes freer.

Practice the work: Yin yoga with voice (video)

Exercise 15: Poses and voice

Now practice the poses again with the sounds intoned as suggested. These should be intoned for the entire time you are in the pose, which once again is 2 minutes per side.

Deer pose, the sound released and intoned is LAHM.

Dragon pose, the sound released and intoned is VARM.

Spinal twist, the sound released and intoned is RAHM.

Supported fish, the sound released and intoned is YAHM.

Sphynx pose, the sound released and intoned is HALM.

Child's pose, the sound released and intoned is OM.

Dangling pose to standing-up pose, the sound is AH.

You will notice I have added voice and speech with each pose or asanas. You can do these poses for longer than the times I have suggested, especially when you start to explore sounds further. However, do take care when coming out of the poses as the fascia and tissue you have worked on will be very released. Afterwards take in some water and notice how you feel in your mind, body and voice. These are all floor-based poses, although I have included one dangling-standing pose as our final pose. Further to that you may have noticed that we were working on the chakras, or wheels of energy, but more of that later in Chapter 7.

Understand the work: Intoning and resonance

Intoning (to recite with little rise or fall in the voice; usually on one pitch/note) whilst in the poses offers you the chance to connect with the breath and further into sound. You may even notice a stronger sense of resonance (how phonation or sound is increased and intensified by the air-filled cavities through which it passes during exhalation) as the body has been open and free allowing a fuller investigation into the power of the breath through extended periods of these poses. You can follow these videos to keep up your daily practice.

Exercise 16: Poses and text

Look at the passage below from Shakespeare's play *Richard III*. Try using some or all of the poses above with the text listed, making your way to standing pose. In brackets I am suggesting where to change poses.

Act 1 Scene 1

Richard III

(deer right side)

Now is the winter of our discontent
Made glorious summer by this son of York;
And all the clouds that lour'd upon our house
In the deep bosom of the ocean buried.

(deer left side)

Now are our brows bound with victorious wreaths;
Our bruised arms hung up for monuments;
Our stern alarums changed to merry meetings,
Our dreadful marches to delightful measures.
Grim-visaged war hath smooth'd his wrinkled front;

(low-flying dragon right side)

And now, instead of mounting barbed steeds
To fright the souls of fearful adversaries,
He capers nimbly in a lady's chamber
To the lascivious pleasing of a lute.

(low-flying dragon left side)

But I, that am not shaped for sportive tricks,
Nor made to court an amorous looking glass;
I, that am rudely stamp'd, and want love's majesty
To strut before a wanton ambling nymph;

(supported fish pose)

I, that am curtail'd of this fair proportion,
Cheated of feature by dissembling nature,
Deformed, unfinish'd, sent before my time
Into this breathing world, scarce half made up,
And that so lamely and unfashionable
That dogs bark at me as I halt by them;

(sphinx pose)

Why, I, in this weak piping time of peace,
Have no delight to pass away the time,
Unless to spy my shadow in the sun,
And descant on mine own deformity:

(child's pose)

And therefore, since I cannot prove a lover,
To entertain these fair well-spoken days,
I am determined to prove a villain
And hate the idle pleasures of these days.

(dangling pose to upright pose)

Plots have I laid, inductions dangerous,
By drunken prophecies, libels and dreams,
To set my brother Clarence and the King
In deadly hate, the one against the other:
And if King Edward be as true and just
As I am subtle, false and treacherous,
This day should Clarence closely be mew'd up,
About a prophecy, which says that 'G'
Of Edward's heirs the murderer shall be.
Dive, thoughts, down to my soul:
here Clarence comes.

Practice the work: Spine, back and shoulders

Figure 1.2 Bowtie.

Exercise 17: Bowtie pose

Start off in sphinx pose, allow a few deep breaths, then lying flat take your left hand under the right elbow and your right arm under the left elbow with palms facing upwards. Let your head fall to a block, cushion or bolster, or you may want the head to drop to the floor. Make a conscious effort to move the shoulders downwards and away from the ears in a downward motion.

Inhale and exhale a few times in this position. This is a great upper back and shoulder stretch and improves posture by creating awareness of the shoulders and the shoulder girdle.

Now hum for 1 minute.

This works on stretching and soothing tight shoulders and upper back. Now breathe freely into the ribs, belly and back. This pose is good for opening the back of the lungs and works on the trapezius muscles and shoulder girdle.

Figure 1.3 Eagle arms.

Exercise 18: Eagle arms pose

Sitting upright, or standing in neutral posture, with your arms facing out in front, swing your left arm under your right arm, crossing at the elbows and wrists. The aim is to get palm to palm, facing each other, but take this slowly. Bring the elbows down. Now breathe freely into the ribs, belly and back, then hum for 1 minute.

This pose is a wonderful way to open the shoulder blades, moving the scapula away from the spine.

Exercise 19: Thread the needle pose

Starting in tabletop position with the knees under the hips, lift your left arm up to the sky on an inward breath, and on the outward breath bring your arm through your right arm, resting on the posterior side of your left shoulder. Then bring your right arm and stretch this forwards. Watch that your hips stay aligned and do not fall towards the side you are working on. Stay here for up to 2 minutes then change sides, humming for 2 minutes each side.

Figure 1.4 Thread the needle.

This pose is a gentle twist to the spine, bringing greater mobility to the thoracic spine, and reduces upper back and neck tension and finally opens the shoulders chest, arms and back and neck.

Exercise 20: Neutral posture and text

Now stand in neutral pose and speak the Shakespeare sonnet listed.

> Shakespeare sonnet number 7
>
> Lo, in the orient when the gracious light
> Lifts up his burning head, each under eye
> Doth homage to his new-appearing sight,
> Serving with looks his sacred majesty.
> And having climbed the steep-up heavenly hill,
> Resembling strong youth in his middle age,
> Yet mortal looks adore his beauty still,
> Attending on his golden pilgrimage.
> But when from highmost pitch, with weary care,
> Like feeble age he reeleth from the day,

The eyes, fore duteous, now converted are
From his low tract and look another way:
So, thou, thyself outgoing in thy noon,
Unlooked on diest unless thou get a son.
How does your spine feel?
Has the spine and yoga work affected your posture and standing pose?
Are you aware of your spine?

Cool-down – body scan and mindfulness script

Feel the work: Cool-down and be present

I have included a script for a class member or the tutor to read out so that everyone else in the room can explore a body scan meditation. This body scan script can be used as the cool-down in a quiet space or with some gentle music.

Exercise 21: Cool-down and be present – body scan script

Sit or lie somewhere comfortably. Now take a deep breath in through the nose and out through the mouth fully, try this a few times, in through the nose and out through the mouth. Tuning into your body, create a mindful approach to the body scan that allows you to notice your thoughts, understand the distractions you place on yourself and will allow you to explore creatively your voice and body by noticing and understanding what it means to be 'present'. The spirit of true co-operation between yourself, your fellow actors and your director in the rehearsal space or studio will allow you greater possibilities in communication, integrity and truthfulness.

Breathe in through the nose and out of the mouth. Focus the mind. Focus on top of the head, breath in and out, feel as if the top of the head is floating upwards.

Do you feel any pressure?

Notice the feeling in your forehead, your face, your eyebrows, your eyes, nose and mouth as you bring your attention downwards. Take a deep breath and let it out. Bring the awareness to the sides of your head near your temples and then move your awareness down into your ears. Bring your awareness towards your face, your nose, breathing nice and easy. Feel the nose as the breath enters in and out.

Now move the awareness down to the mouth, the jaw, the lips, let the jaw gently relax. Bring awareness down into your throat. Now bring the awareness to the back of your neck. Bring your focus down to your shoulders, feel the possibility of letting go of your shoulders. Feel the weight of your arms and let go resting your arms on your knees. Think about both arms and elbows, your wrists and into the hands and fingers. And breathe.

Bring your awareness to the ribcage, chest and back as you inhale and exhale. Move your awareness to your upper abdomen and the sensations of your belly.

Is your belly tense or relaxed?

Bring your awareness further down towards your lower back and lower stomach. Bring your awareness to your hips and pelvis. Now move your awareness down to your thighs and feel the heaviness and strength in your thighs. Continue your awareness into your knees. Continue moving your mind downwards towards your lower legs, to your calf muscles, then your ankles, feel the sensation of your ankles. Now bring awareness all the way down to your feet, feel your toes, the soles of your feet, now your awareness has scanned on your whole body. Notice how you feel.

When you feel ready wriggle your toes and fingers. Open your eyes and bring yourself into sitting upright or standing and being present.

Understand the work: Being present and mindful

What do we really mean by the term 'being present'? If I am in the space, of course I must be present. Following many years of being a very adrenal person, in other words full of adrenalin and over-working and constantly talking, I began a lifelong journey in meditation, tai chi and yin yoga. I now come to understand the true meaning of the term 'being present'. I now notice the moment.

However, to be truly present requires you to listen but not engage, to be alert but not take flight, to notice without judgement. To be honest and have integrity.

Tips for teachers

Meditation and relaxation can support you as a teacher as well as your students. It can be a great start to a session or a calm way to end a class, it can also enhance moments through feedback, develop a critical understanding of self in the work and in the space. It can also be used as homework which you can suggest, as there are plenty of online resources such as 'headspace.com'. To take this further you could suggest that students create their own type of cool-down body scan meditation, letting your students develop a practice to share with the group, whether it is pre-recorded or live, with music that is appropriate. By getting them to prepare for this allows them a choice to engage with a softer yet clear quality of vocal delivery.

Suggested texts

Bernard Snyder, *Still Standing* (2016), Charlestan: Palmetto Publishing Group.
William Carlos Williams, 'The friend who just stands', *Collected Poems*, Vol 1 (2018), Manchester: Carcanet Classics.
William Stafford, '*The Way It Is*' (2006), Minneapolis: Graywolf Press.
May Sarton, *Meditation in Sunlight* (2014), New York: Open Road Media.

Further reading

Bain, K. (2015), *The Principles of Movement*, London: Oberon Books.

Bainbridge, Cohen B. (1994), *Sensing Feeling and Action*, Berkeley, CA: North Atlantic Books.

Carey, D., and Carey, R. Clark (2008), *Vocal Arts Workbook and DVD*, London: Methuen Drama.

Langer, Ellen J. (2014), *Mindfulness*, Boston, MA: Da Capo Lifelong Books.

Linklater, K. (2006), *Freeing the Natural Voice*, London: Nick Hern Books.

Long, R. (2008), *The Key Poses of Yoga*, Baldwinsville, NY: Bandha Yoga Publication.

Nicholls, C. (2008), *Body, Breath and Being: A new guide to the Alexander Technique*, Hove: D and B Publishers.

Reinhardt, K. (2018), *Yin Yoga*, London: DK Penguin Random House.

Shakespeare, William (1995), *The Sonnets and A Lovers Complaint*, London: Penguin Classics.

Shakespeare, William (2010), *The Complete Works of Shakespeare: The Arden Shakespeare*, London: Bloomsbury.

2 Breath – Through Michael Chekhov, Inspired by Tai Chi

> A journey of a thousand miles begins with a single step. CHINESE PROVERB

Imagination is more important than knowledge. Knowledge is limited. Imagination encircles the world. ALBERT EINSTEIN

Breath meaning:

1. Gasp for breath.
2. Breathe life into it.
3. Breath of fresh air.

Introduction

In this chapter we will explore the connection of the breath to voice and body, capturing the essence and exploring some exercises of the actor training of Michael Chekhov, and finally working breath into sound. Michael Chekhov sought to create 'sensitivity of the body to the psychological creative impulses' as mentioned in his book *To the Actor*. This spoke to me as a student actor, and I sought to bring this into my teaching of voice many years ago. This chapter will deepen your understanding of your breathing muscles, for relaxation, for social voice and for performance. Managing your breath will also establish the relationship to thought and body, and the efficiency of your breath in relation to one or more acting or movement techniques. This chapter is designed to support the work of Michael Chekhov's acting methods. We will begin by exploring and adopting breath in a variety of ways including the movements of inspired tai chi as a warm-up, before investigating Chekhov's acting methodology and breath.

What is the key to good breath support? Certainly, harnessing the breath to the thought process, and thinking through to the end of the line makes sense. As actors we can learn the lines of text, underestimating the connection to the breath. *But how do we manage breath support on long sentences?* Well, the short answer is working on your breath management to increase the ability to employ your breath with greater efficiency. *Can you increase your lung capacity?* Technically no, you cannot, however you can manage the breath in your lungs with greater control. The lines in your chosen text need to be considered as thoughts or intentions, to aid the support on the intake of breath as you manage both objectives and intentions.

The main aim of the breathing muscles is to keep us alive, and where we see this in action is the very first breath a baby takes as they enter the world.

In my voice training for actors, I select exercises inspired by tai chi movements to manage and sustain the breath into the body, as it supports investigations into imagery, radiates and receives energies, connects the voice and body with control and ease, and consolidates a set of fully integrated voice and movement skills, all the things that connect breath to Michael Chekhov. The health benefits are widely reported using true tai chi, in that it aids performance anxiety, decreases the sympathetic activation, can improve mood and wellbeing, helps better sleep hygiene, and when used with deep breathing, helps stimulate the body's own detox lymphatic system too.

There are many different approaches to exploring voice and movement and I have, through my own practice, discovered the philosophy of inspired tai chi that has enabled my students to explore their vocal range, breath capacity, volume, stamina and dynamic power. This can become a wonderful warm-up that extends to a daily practice whether performing or not.

The inspired tai chi breathing and movement sequence on the video has been heavily adapted so that the names are in English, and the sequence is a widely exaggerated version of inspired tai chi that suggests a flow like quality.

Breath and distinctive styles of breathing

Feel the work: Breathing and distinctive styles

Exercise 1

Let us first explore assorted styles of breathing techniques. Stand in neutral posture as explored in Chapter 1 and notice your breathing as it enters and leaves the body. Practice this for 1 minute.

Now sit on a chair and continue to feel the breath as it enters and leaves the body. Practice this for 1 minute.

Now try the same again lying in semi-supine and explore the breath as it enters and leaves the body. Practice this for 1 minute.

Do you observe any changes in how you breathe from standing to sitting to lying down?

Observe the ways to breathe in the exercises listed, so that your imagination is fired, and your breathing is stimulated by your choices.

Exercise 2: Breath 365

Now sitting or standing in neutral posture, breathe in through the nose and out through the mouth. Attempt to breathe in for

3 seconds, out for 6 seconds, and manage this five times in 1 minute.

This conscious breathing exercise of controlling your breath can calm nerves, make you aware of your breathing and allow you to understand the relationship between the in breath and the out breath. Observe how you feel.

Exercise 3: Ujjayi breath or ocean breath

Lying in semi-supine, or sitting upright, take a breath in through the nose, and on the outward breath allow the subtle construction of the glottis to produce a hissing sound like the ocean. A wonderful way to think about the sound you are creating is to imagine you are steaming up a mirror with your exhalation of breath. Try this a few times and observe how you feel.

Understand the work

This kind of breath work involves slightly constricting the throat to produce a long breath that covers the glottis, by bringing the vocal cords to a narrow opening, enabling this small passageway to allow the breath to lengthen and the 'ocean sound' to be produced by the vibrating across the vocal cords.

Exercise 4: Alternate nostril breathing

In a sitting position on a chair or cross legged on the floor, with your right hand, place your forefinger and middle finger in the middle of your forehead.

Now place your thumb against the right nostril and breathe in through the left nostril.

Now place your ring finger against the left nostril and breathe out through your right nostril.

Alternate between closing off one nostril at a time and breathing in through one nostril and out through the other. Try this for 1 minute.

Research shows that right-nostril breathing increases oxygen levels in the left prefrontal cortex. The left-nostril breathing reduces oxygen in the right hemisphere of the brain. There is greater airflow through the right nostril and improved cardiorespiratory functions and psychological stress. Observe how you feel.

Exercise 5: Humming bee breath

Sitting upright, block out sound with your fingers in your ears. Inhale through the nose and exhale through the nose on the hum sound. Its purpose is to stimulate better oxygen flow and can support the sound, allowing some auditory feedback. Observe how you feel.

Inspired tai chi and breath into sound

Feel the work: Breath through inspired tai chi

Warm-up and breath work through tai chi inspired movements. Which you will also find on the videos for all the sequences.

Exercise 6:

Sequence 1 (the three treasures)

Gather the chi or breath.

Send the chi or breath out to the world.

Send the chi or breath up to the universe.

The above exercise explores breath and movement.

Understand the work: The three treasures

Using inspired tai chi allows you to explore movement, breath and technique, which contribute to the wellbeing of the body and mind. The chi is considered to be the life force, the energy, the prana or spirit. It does not matter what you believe, so long as you feel the breath entering and leaving your body for the full extension of the movements.

Exercise 7: Repeat sequence 1 (the three treasures) with breath released on an /f/ or /s/ sh

The following exercises can also be found on the videos:

Exercise 8: The archer for 2 minutes
Exercise 9: Separate the clouds for 2 minutes
Exercise 10: Gaze up at the moon for 2 minutes
Exercise 11: Stroke horse's back for 2 minutes
Exercise 12: Push dragon away for 2 minutes
Exercise 13: Fingers in sand for 2 minutes
Exercise 14: Golf ball swing for 2 minutes
Exercise 15: The crow for 2 minutes
Exercise 16: Part horse's mane for 1 minute each side
Exercise 17: Single whip for 1 minute each side
Exercise 18: Spread eagle wings for 1 minute each side

Now end the full sequence with the three treasures for 2 minutes.

Place your hands on your belly and breathe in through the nose and out through the mouth. Notice how you feel.

Understand the work: Through inspired tai chi

This inspired tai chi practice promotes balance and harmony and allows you to develop breath in movement and sound in movement. It also sets up a daily practise where you have moved from the neutral of standing into movement in action, and an awareness of bodily sensations.

Using the video to explore voice and body in movement allows us to see how balance effects posture in space. *Are you able to keep good alignment when working through the exercises?* Try to breathe with fluidity. It also allows time to feel how your body moves and reflect through posture and alignment when in constant flow. Good posture is only useful if you can move. It is not often you will stand still on the stage, and if you did, how might your back and legs be affected?

The inspired tai chi breath and sound work has been adapted to support the voice work rather than the quiet work of the original or traditional quiet practice of tai chi. However, this will give you an understanding not only of the original and authentic practice but also of the enormous benefit of combining such a traditional-based philosophy of body work and breath into sound and movement.

The purpose is to improve balance, increase strength in the legs, knees and hips and reduce stress.

Practice the work: Sounds and inspired tai chi (video)

Here are some sounds that are suggested, although you may wish to create your own sounds, and the video may offer some further sounds for you to explore.

Sequence 2 with sound

The archer for 1 minute. The sound could be a sustained /f/.

Separate the clouds for 1 minute. The sound could be a sustained /s/.

Gaze up at the moon for 1 minute. The sound could be an OO vowel.

Stroke horse's back for 1 minute. The sound could be an AH vowel.

Push dragon away for 1 minute. The sound could be a sustained SH.

Fingers in sand for 1 minute. The sound could be a sustained /V/ followed by a quick /f/s/ or sh.

Golf ball swing for 1 minute. The sound could be a sustained /f/ or /s/.

The crow for 1 minute. The sound is ft like shooting an arrow sound, followed by a sustained sh.

Part horse's mane for 1 minute. The sound could be a HUH or HO.

Single whip for 1 minute. The sound is HI-YAH or a YA HA.

Spread eagle wings for 1 minute. The sound is AYE-YA or a YOU HA.

These later exercises in the video you will see explore sound, creating breath, voice and body interconnectedness.

Tips for teachers

The video and information are inspired tai chi exercises that I have adapted to include in my voice teaching, from tai chi sequences which are different from true tai chi, to create a daily practice. If your students would like to gain insight into the true authentic tai chi there are a list of websites and organisations that you will see in Appendix 2 that you could explore further.

The first sequence, the three treasures, I recommend doing daily as this creates a mood of self-sought discipline which can be a positive way to start the class. The further practice sequence could be given as homework to develop your students' own practice. If the moves are not 'right' this is fine as the principle is to enhance breath and body work initially, then moving to body and sound work. This can be explored as homework as part of a 'flipped' class and to be realised further with sound in class.

Breathing muscles and anatomy

Feel the work: Belly breath

Accessing the breath through the belly.

Exercise 19: Belly bowl exercise

Lie on the floor on your front with your forehead gently resting on your hands so that you engage with a long-relaxed neck. Relax your thighs, buttocks, legs and feet, and breathe.

Breathe into your belly and feel your belly on the floor as you imagine carving a bowl with your stomach into the floor. Try this for a few minutes. Notice how you feel.

Can you feel your belly expand into the floor?

Explore further, allow the belly bowl to expand and the ribs to expand further sideways and outwards, feeling the sway of movement as those bigger breaths on inhalation and exhalation are realised.

Now lie on your left side, close your eyes, and place your hand on your belly, still imagining the bowl you are creating. Notice

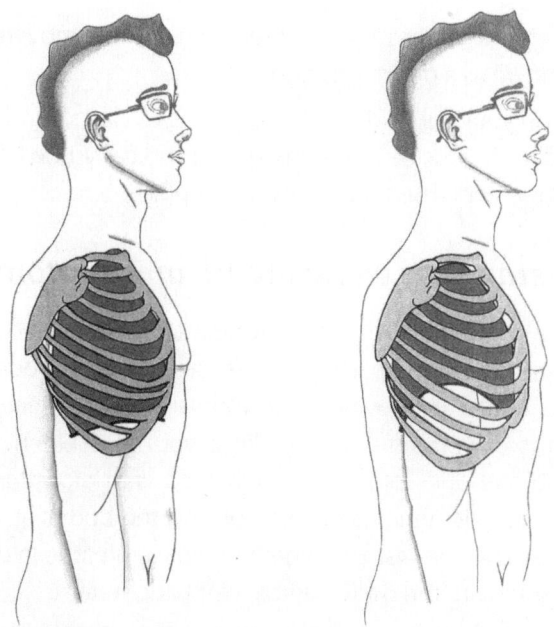

Figure 2.1 The diaphragm: showing the falling (A) and rising (B) on inhalation and exhalation.

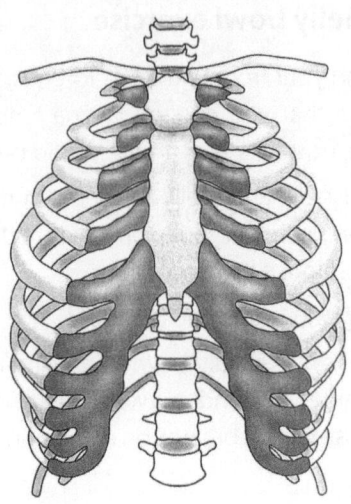

Figure 2.2 The ribcage.

how you feel and observe your breathing and the movements. This is known as a digest position.

Now lie on your right side, keeping your eyes closed, and place your hand on your belly, still imagining the belly bowl, falling towards the floor. This is known as a rest position.

Understand the work: Breath and anatomy

As you lie on your left side, you may hear some gurgling sounds. These are not hunger pains, they are the sounds of your large intestine contents moving into your smaller intestine. This position is a wonderful way to lie if you have eaten a late meal and feel uncomfortable, it will help with digestion. The parasympathetic nervous system controls the body's ability to relax, known as the rest and digest, when we breathe in deeply it helps stimulate the body's detox lymphatic system.

We breathe in and out roughly 12–20 breaths per minute at rest. We breathe in and out roughly 940–960 breaths an hour at rest.

We breathe in and out roughly 20,000–23,000 times per day. (You do not stop breathing at night!)

We breathe in and out roughly 8,409,600 per year at rest.

How many breaths have you taken in your lifetime so far?

Of course, we breathe much more frequently during exercise, movement, body work, and of course accessing distinctive vocal and physical characteristics through acting, as we consciously choose what may be useful for a character's emotions. For example when expressing anger, fear, pain, love or joy, all of which affects the breath.

When we breathe consciously, we can use breath to change our emotional state: from the feeling of being angry or frustrated, to slowing down our breathing to become calm, relaxed and reasonable. So, we can adjust the breath to use as a tool to access our emotions consciously as an actor.

Breathing happens by the movement of the diaphragm in a downwards motion. The diaphragm is a dome-, umbrella- or parachute-shaped muscle (depending on your imagination) which sits at the bottom of the chest, below your lungs and heart, separating the abdomen from the chest. It is attached to your sternum (at a bone in the middle of your chest known as the xiphoid process of the sternum). When you breathe in (inhale) the diaphragm flattens and contracts. When you breathe out (exhale) the diaphragm relaxes and pushes air out of the lungs via the nose and mouth causing the diaphragm to go back to its original shape.

This involuntary muscle needs help to move downwards and that help comes from the abdomen. When you release the muscles in the abdomen there is more space for the diaphragm to move downwards. When we take an 'in breath', that downwards movement increases the volume in the chest. This lowers the air pressure in the lungs which fill up with air to equalise the air pressure. The 'in breaths' (inhalation) purpose is to oxygenate air to the alveoli (minute air sacs) inside the lungs. The 'out breath' (exhalation) disturbs this sequence of events; the diaphragm moves back up to its dome shape once again and the chest has a smaller volume as air flows from the lungs through the nose and or mouth taking with it the carbon dioxide gas to equalise the pressure once more.

The ribcage houses the vital organs of heart and lungs. It looks like a birdcage or a basket of bony structures, is attached to the thoracic spine and is made up of twenty-four ribs. These are in pairs either side of the spine and there are twelve pairs of ribs. They are numbered as follows:

- 1–7 (seven pairs of true ribs) which are attached to the sternum or breastbone.
- 8–10 (three pairs of false ribs) which are attached to rib 7 at the front.
- 11–12 (two pairs of floating ribs) which are attached to the back of the spine but non-attached at the front.

Understand the work

When we breathe in, the external intercostal muscles of the ribcage are connected to the ribs, causing the ribcage to expand both forwards and sideways. This causes the lungs to expand and so we breathe in. When we breathe out, these external muscles relax while the internal intercostal muscles, which are attached to the inner surfaces of the ribs, help bring everything back to a resting position.

Tips for teachers

This following exercise gives your students permission to let it all hang out. Allow the intestines to flop onto the floor (metaphorically) and create space in the stomach. Notice how this makes them feel, perhaps guiding them to critically think about this, and also notice how much their upper body may move as they work the belly in the opposite way that you would if you were standing. Ask them to consciously push out the belly on the in breath. Exploring the breath beyond lying down really focuses the body to react to how we hold the breath or use our bodies differently. The rest and digest elements of breathing on the left side or the right side as listed exposes the students to their guts and large and small intestines. Hearing how deep breath work affects the space inside the stomach is key to recognising how a held stomach affects a held sound and voice. A further exercise is to ask your students to work out how many times they have breathed in and out today, in a week, in their lifetime so far. Perhaps get them to do their families too. This can become a breath and maths equation.

Practice the work: Further belly bowl
Exercise 20

Lie in belly bowl position, on your left side and spend up to 3 minutes in this position to access your breath consciously, continuing to create a bowl shape in the floor.

Figure 2.3 Blowing up a balloon.

Now move onto your right side, breathing in and out for 3 minutes, and place your hand on your belly and notice how you feel. Each side should be up to 3 minutes.

Feel the work: Balloon breath
Exercise 21: Imagination and creativity

Hold your hands out in front of you and imagine you have an unblown balloon in your hands.

Imagine you are blowing up a balloon in stages. Try to make the shape of the balloon long and thin or round and fat. Imagine the shape and colour of the balloon.

Allow the balloon to collapse and see this in the shape of your hands.

Now try blowing up the balloon again with different blasts of air, for example blow hard and fast, or slow and sustained.

Notice the small but intense sharp blast of breath as you blow up the balloon.

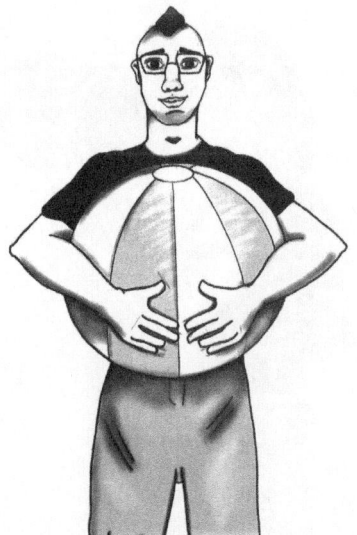

Figure 2.4 Blowing up a beach ball.

Now try blowing up a balloon again using one long breath – as you are blowing up the balloon see how far the shape you intend to make grows.

Did you manage to make a full shape?

Try this a few more times, each time allowing the imaginary balloon to collapse.

Exercise 22: Beach ball breath

Now try the same exercise again only this time explore the size of a large beach ball, and its colours, then hold the breath.

Now slowly release the breath and imagine you have stuck a pin in your beach ball and see this large beach ball collapse.

Practice the work: Further work on breath

Exercise 23

Place your hand on your clavicle or collar bone and just breathe in and out. Notice the subtle movement.

Now place your hands firmly on your ribcage and inhale. Notice how your ribs swing out on the in breath.

Now slowly release the breath (out breath) and the hands will follow the ribs as they gently swing back to a neutral position. Try this a few times and feel the expansion of the ribs.

Exercise 24: Accessing the breath

Lieing on the floor in semi supine, try the same exercise again only imagine you have a small feather on your lips that you are trying to remove with every outward breath.

Use the /fff/ sound to remove the feather.

Try this a few times fff, fff, fff, fff, fff.

Now imagine you have a bow and arrow and are releasing the bow to the ceiling on the ft sound as often as you can ft, ft, ft.

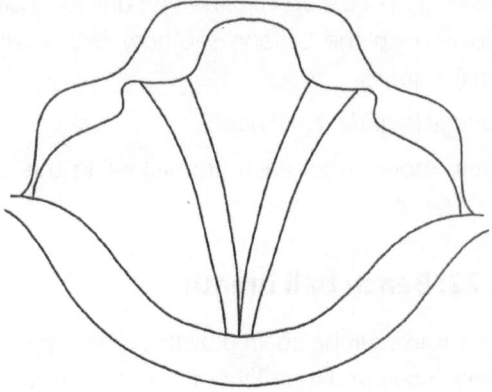

Figure 2.5 The vocal folds open.

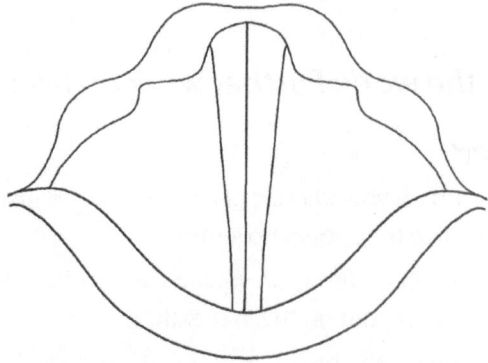

Figure 2.6 The vocal folds closed.

Next, as you continue to lie on the floor imagine you are a machine that vibrates to create a painting on the ceiling with the v sound.

Understand the work: Breath and phonation

Voicing sounds or 'phonation' is generated when the vocal folds, or vocal cords as they are sometimes known, vibrate. They sit inside the larynx and there is a collective integrated orchestra coming together to produce sound. First the conductor *(the brain)* tells the lungs *(first violinist)* that air needs to be inhaled.

They make sure the air reaches the *(second violinist)* space between the vocal folds or glottis, then they nod to the laryngeal muscles *(the rest of the orchestra)* to work together *(in concert)* to bring the vocal folds together *(trumpets)* (adduction). As air pressure builds beneath those adducted folds the *(trumpet player)* ensures they are blown apart. When the air pressure drops across the glottis space, the vocal folds work together again until the entire process repeats itself, making a clean and unmistakable sound of togetherness, much like an orchestra.

The breath management can alter the sound of the voice, such as whispering or creating a vocal mood. This would mean the vocal folds may not be fully adducted creating an unvoiced but creative sound. Breath is everything.

When we are at rest and breathing in and out, our breath for life is unconscious. It becomes conscious when we must do a task such as blowing up a balloon or beach ball. *How does your breath affect the long speech you may have? Or the volume you may need? Or the intention behind the lines?* This is when we become more conscious of our breathing and how to best manage it.

You already know how to breathe, you have been doing it your whole life, but to consciously engage with your breathing takes time to recognise the impulse and trust the work to fully allow your breath to serve your voice, volume, pitch, resonance and articulation.

Tips for teachers

In the rollercoaster exercise, I normally set this in class with students sitting on chairs in pairs in two lines facing the front of the room. The students should have their eyes closed and know they are safe. I guide them through the excitement of the exercise so that they may end up shouting or screaming as the excitement takes them over. (I may even use a folder to waft up and down each student's face so that it feels like the wind.) It is one their favourite exercises to explore breath and excitement. I might suggest saying something as follows:

Now sit on your chair and imagine you are at a fairground and have just got onto a rollercoaster. You are normally afraid of rollercoasters, however today you love them. Imagine that you are slowly rising becoming increasingly vertical and you reach the top and you stay there. Then whoosh, the rollercoaster drops fast down. In your mind's eye imagine how you feel, notice your breath. Notice if this exercise affects your heart, head, gut, or other parts of your body.

In each of these exercises we have explored breath in stillness, breath in expansion, by using imagery and finally breath in an imaginary setting such as the fairground. We are exploring breath in a controlled and deliberate way, and in a way that shocks the body. Notice in each of the cases how you feel.

Michael Chekhov through breath and imagination

Introduction

Having worked on breath through the movements of inspired tai chi as a warm-up, and some exercises on using the imagination, I want to share with you the principles of using breath, imagination, radiating, image centres and voice, to serve the acting work of Michael Chekhov. It is important to state that voice training and acting and movement methodologies go hand in hand, and I have used many that work for me as a vocal coach, an actor, acting teacher and a director.

Michael Chekhov believed that the actor's greatest gifts are imagination, intuition and artistic vision, and that the actor's job is to interpret life, conveying meaning and an inner life to the audience. Not to imitate life, but that there should be a sensitivity of body, receptive to creative impulses, through psychological gestures, which the actor's body can develop from the inside out. The actor radiates the inner life of the character using the imaginary impulses and radiates the inner life working. The use of the imagination helps to draw upon all manner of thoughts and feelings we embody throughout our life. The actor will draw upon these to create an inner life of the character and incorporate the physical aspects of the character, creating the right atmosphere and sensations. Atmospheres such as hectic, happy, sad or nervous, for example, have an immediate impact on the way we behave and act, which is affected by the breath. The actor can create this atmosphere through imagining the inner impulses. Also, they can employ and select a movement to describe the inner life of sensations and emotions. Of course, ones that are familiar to many actors are the psychological gesture, like emotions and sensations and atmosphere, where a gesture can reflect a person's inner life, desires, feelings, unconscious thoughts, etc., so the actor learns to access these gestures until the gesture required serves the purpose.

Drawing upon the three fundamental areas of Chekhov's work I employ his use of directions, gestures and the relationship to the heart, the head, the gut and the groin, to apply the psychological aspects of a character, by observing the breath, then sound, and finally, text.

Feel the work: Directions (video)
Exercise 25: Forward direction and voice (video)

Stand in neutral posture and centre your weight, remind yourself of the tripod.

Observe your breathing.

Now bring the weight to the front of the foot. Notice if this is a natural place for you or your character. Put your whole attention into the front part of your body.

Do the feelings of breathing change?

Now bring the energy so far forward that you have the impulse to move forward, walking a few paces, or begin to jog or run. Notice the impulse, the energy and the breath.

Return to neutral and reset the body.

Forward direction can imply many thoughts, such as 'being ahead', 'on the front foot' 'forward thinking', 'focused'.

Now try the same forward movement, while producing the sound OH, or you can use another vowel sound of your choice.

What do you notice about the breath?

What do you notice about the pitch?

What do you notice about the intention, the mood or the character?

Practice the work: Forward direction

Continue to stand in a neutral pose, then bring your weight towards the front of your body. Observe the air around the front of your body and face, being aware of any sensations.

Now move forward slightly onto the front of your foot. Radiate energy in the front of your body. Notice if this is a natural place for you to radiate, or if it is useful for the character you are playing. Place your whole attention into the front part of your body. Observe your breath. Notice the inhalation and exhalation. Maintain that shift of weight onto the front of the toes and body, without standing on tiptoes. Notice if you are holding your breath.

Now imagine you are on a platform waiting for a train as it pulls you forward, and you want to be first on the train. Find the impulse to move your body forward into the space, without running. Stop, then wait for the impulse in the front of the body and move again. Notice the breath.

Is the breath coming fast or slow, high or low in the body? Keep exploring this action of moving forward.

Reset the neutral pose after each direction.

Now a take a gasp or inhale as you propel yourself forward.

What does this do to your inner monologue?

How are you feeling?

How would the character you are playing feel being propelled forward?

Let out a sigh.

Now create the sound OH as you move forward on an impulse.

Next speak the word 'yes' as you move forward on an impulse.

Finally speak the word 'no' as you move forward on an impulse.

Now adopt some text you already know. Notice how the exercise affects the pitch and pace, the imagination and the breath. You may feel your character radiate from its core centre.

Finally, continuing to speak a line of text, observe the sensation, notice if it is an impulse or determination, or the sensation that creates an impulse to move forward.

Does this offer any clues into the character you are playing? Try speaking the words of your text propelling yourself forward.

Now come back to neutral pose and reset and register all the sensations and thoughts.

Exercise 26: Backward direction (video)

Stand in a neutral pose, then register your weight and think of the tripod.

Now bring the weight to the back of the foot and legs and register the impulse to step backwards.

How does it affect the breath?

Now say a few lines of your text moving backwards.

What does it do to the character and their lines?

The character may have feelings of regret, left behind, stuck in the past. The energy can appear to be indirect. The breath and pitch can often be affected in the lower range of notes, as the impulse takes you backwards. Notice your breath.

Practice the work: Backward direction

Continue to stand in a neutral pose, and reset your centre of gravity, then centre your weight. Observe the air sensations around the back of your body.

Allow the impulse to move you slightly onto the back of your foot as you feel the sensation in the back of your body. Notice if this is a natural place for you or your character. Put your whole attention into the back part of your body. Observe your breath. *Are you holding your breath?* Notice the inhalation and exhalation. Maintain that shift of weight onto the back of the heels and body, without falling off balance.

Now imagine you have been pushed backwards, feel the impulse, and notice the breath.

Stop, then wait for the impulse in the back of the body and move again. Notice the breath.

Is the breath coming fast or slow, high or low in the body? Keep trying this action of moving backwards but do reset the neutral pose each time.

Now make the breath audible as you move backwards, creating a sensation in the body.

Now a take a gasp or inhale as you propel yourself backwards.

What does this do to your inner monologue? How are you feeling? How would the character you are playing feel being pushed backwards?

Allow an impulse to move you backwards and let out a sigh.

Allow the impulse to move you backwards and let out a sound of /OH/ or AH.

Next, allow the impulse to move you backwards and speak the word YES.

Now exploring the backward impulse say the word NO.

Now using the same text as before, speak and feel the impulse to move backwards.

Does this help your character?

Is it the kind of choice that would support the character?

Does backward direction help you with their impulses?

Exercise 27: Upward direction and voice (video)

Stand in a neutral pose centring your weight.

Now bring the energy upwards so that it feels like you are lifting your heels off the floor, your head is being pulled upwards through your shoulders, hands, arms, eyebrows, etc. Put your attention to the upward energy.

Now speak your text and notice any sensations of the upward feeling. *What does it do to the breath?*

The character may have feelings of hope, excitement, heaven, sky, ceiling, moving up in the world; the energy can be seen as positive.

Pitch as well as breath is often affected and you may create higher notes, just observe this, rather than impose.

Practice the work

Once again stand in neutral pose and feel the energy of the whole body lifting upwards whilst your feet are still on the ground. Bring your mind to the crown of your head and feel what happens to your whole body.

On the upward impulse, let out a sigh.

On the upward impulse, let out a sound of OH.

Next, on the upward impulse speak the word YES.

Now on the upward impulse speak the word NO.

Now vocalise a sound, or words your character would say, or a well rehearsed piece of text.

This sensation can often suggest positivity, or head in the clouds, or up-beat, or joy and lightness.

What are the sensations that are suggested to you and your character?

In these directions have you noticed a change in breath and energy?

You may feel that pitch is affected. Enjoy the sensations of discovery.

Exercise 28: Downward direction (video)

Stand in a neutral pose, then feel the weight and energy move downwards. Notice how different it may feel to the upward sensation.

Now speak your text and notice any sensations of the downward feeling.

The character may have feelings of being depressed, low, down in the dumps, feeling flat, or they could be stubborn, or are grounded.

What does it do to the breath?

Notice if the pitch is lower in the downward direction. Notice the sensation.

Notice your breath, feel the impulse rather than impose.

Practice the work further

Bring yourself back to the neutral pose and feel your weight move downwards, feel the weight in your legs.

Feel your feet grounded down without forcing. Bring your energy into the feet, hips and knees and notice the breath.

On a downward impulse, let out a sigh.

On the downward impulse, let out a sound of OH or AH.

Now say the word YES.

Next try the word NO.

Now let out a sound of words your character would say, or some text.

What sensations have you noticed?

This down direction can feel heavy or dull but can also feel grounded or controlled. Understand the sensations in your body and the effect on your breath and emotions.

Exercise 29: Right direction

Stand in neutral pose then shift your weight to the right foot very slightly. You are not trying to balance on one foot, it is merely a millimetre of energy to the right direction.

Now speak your text and notice the energy of the lines whilst leaning slightly to the right.

Now use gestures that come from the right side of your body.

Is the sensation the same or different from your character?

Perhaps say a few lines as you walk towards the right of the stage.

Notice the pitch and breath, is it affected on the right side as you speak and gesture?

Exercise 30: Left direction

Stand in neutral pose, then shift your weight to the left foot very slightly. You are not trying to balance on one foot, it is merely a millimetre of energy to the left direction.

Now speak your text and notice the energy of the lines whilst leaning slightly to the left.

Now use gestures that come from the left side of your body.

Is the sensation the same or different from you and your character?

Perhaps say a few lines walking towards the left side of the stage or room, your body is keen to move off in that direction.

What do you notice about how your character feels?

Is your starting note different from your right side?

Exercise 31: Back story and sensations, 30 minutes

Stand in neutral pose, and with your back against a wall, reset your energy centre, then centre your weight, accessing your breath to calm and centre yourself. Allow your body in standing pose to feel relaxed. Close your eyes for a moment and experience the sensation of the back of your body against the wall. Alternatively, if wall space is limited, use the sensation of leaning back onto your heels and feeling the back space in this way.

Put your body as much as you can against the wall, making contact from head to foot with the wall. Relax the face, jaw, neck, lips and any frown.

Now imagine your first memory (you can try this as yourself or the character). This exercise is powerful and creates a series of images and memories to come flooding into your conscious mind from your unconscious mind.

Close your eyes to focus your breathing.

Now open your eyes and keep them looking straight ahead, but soften the gaze.

Now begin walking slowly forwards. As you do this exercise allow your imagination to think about your past or your character's past, the past of the world, which may be significant moments in your character's journey to today. Images may flood in from your past that may be significant, or overwhelming, so see them and acknowledge them, breathe through them, and move a step forwards. Do not stand still in them as you must continue to move forwards. As you see the images come flooding in vocalise a breath or sigh, quietly to yourself- or notice the breath within each memory.

Take the time to walk across the entire length of the room imagining that the wall opposite is right now. Today.

Whatever images flood into your mind, whether significant or not, they will have formed who you are and how you navigate the world.

This is the same for any character you play. Allow yourself the time to truly learn who your character is.

Whilst in this exercise notice the breath and how much it is affected by the images coming through.

Observe the breath as you move forwards whilst recognising the back of the space – the behind space, the past, the history.

Once you have crossed the room moving forwards but sensing the back, let out an audible breath, then a word.

Vocalise a sigh of the sound of joy.

Vocalise a sound of pain.

Vocalise the sound of the word yes.

Vocalise the sound of the word no.

When working in the back space it can create sensations of great moments of joy or pain or mistakes, or regret, or loneliness or loss or even guilt; notice and observe this. The imagery you are discovering about yourself is also helpful on how to create your characters back story, how it radiates the past, and allows you the actor to step into their reality.

Now come back to a neutral pose and reset your centre and notice how you feel. This imagery-based exercise is immensely powerful and incorporates both mind and body, breath and even spirit. Notice the characters who may inhabit space that is reflective, looking backwards.

Exercise 32: Full combo of directions, sensations and voice

Now try being playful with your text, using your breath exhalation to explore all the directions, then speak a line of text and observe what happens when the impulse to move you forward or back, up or down, or to one side or another. Try many combinations and observe what choices the exercise offers you as an actor.

Exercise 33: Archetypical gestures and vocals

The archetypical gestures are used to explore the basic clear intent of the body. These are the pure gestures. Exploring a release of breath, on each activity, notice what they offer you as an actor. Notice if any emotion or change in breath is attached to the physical action. Notice if there is any psychological impact.

Place or put down something like a book, a pen, a drink, or any object.

Did you hold your breath?

Lift or rise up an object.

Do you hold your breath or let out a sound?

Drag over your shoulders a heavy bag or a heavy object and notice your breath and effort.

Throw something that requires your whole body to engage – observe if your breath is compromised, or you emitted any sound.

Pull something towards you and notice the breath.

Push something away and notice your breath.

Rip or tear and feel your breath as you try this both fast and slow.

Now try the same again using the /ah/ sound.

Finally, do the same gestures again using the text.

What sensations do you notice?

Exercise 34: Psychological gestures

This is described as the connection between your body and your inner life. The form suggests the qualities of the feelings or desires. This gives you an idea of the character's outward feelings. All gestures should incorporate from head to toe, the entire body. The actor externalises an inner want, through a gesture. This can manifest deliberately and habitually or after a while can be an internal gesture and the actor merely must think the gesture. However, the body is always fully involved. Working with a character you have established a connection with to their text or monologue, begin by exploring a gesture that investigates their feelings. The gesture is not fixed so do not feel you are tied to that gesture. If you cannot think of one there are a few examples listed.

- Rub your hands together.
- Thumb and forefinger rubbing.
- Playing with your hair.
- Scratching an imaginary itch on your arm.
- Tap the head or scratch it.
- Place hand on heart.
- Clasp hands near the heart.
- Put hands in the pockets.

Using any one of these gestures or one of your own you have investigated, explore the breath through the character as you continue this motion of the gesture.

Now allow a breath to escape whilst doing the gesture.

Next explore releasing the breath and the gesture.

Now explore the Ah sound and gesture.

And finally, explore the gesture and the rehearsed text.

Notice the sensations.

Now explore with one gesture, using the breath to underpin the text listed to develop an inner life that suggests subtext, inner thoughts and outward physical response.

Understand the work: Gestures and voice

A gesture is a movement, usually the hand or head, to express ideas or meanings. Michael Chekhov uses these to express and access the inner character's life. The behavioural gestures externalise a character's internal thoughts, which can support an actor to make the feelings and thoughts more concrete. It allows actors to stimulate the imagination, constantly refining the gesture until it feels real. Through repetition, the actor will be more deeply connected to the psychological make up of the character.

Exercise 35: Heart, head, gut and groin

Place your hand in one of the four centres listed, it can be on the area or around the area to focus your mind.

Place your hand on your heart.

Now place your hand in the area of your head.

Next place your hand on the area of your gut/stomach.

Finally, place your hand in the area of your lower tummy or groin area.

Now try each of these areas and speak your text and notice the difference in delivery as you speak the text.

Notice what thoughts or feelings this provokes.

Does the principles of the heart, the head, the gut or the groin help support the ideas or intentions of the character?

Understand the work: Heart, head, gut and groin

Heart, head, gut and groin gestures are emotional centres, which can create more nuance and authenticity, supporting the actor to connect with their characters on a deeper level to convey meanings and intentions.

Head characters it seems may draw their energy from the head and the gestures may come from there. They could be big thinkers, analytical, or considered reasonable. The text could be linked to logic or decision making, reasoning, or planning, or calculating.

The character speaking about love speaks from the heart. It might be suggested that those speaking from the heart are full of passion and compassion, joy or pain, have empathy and vulnerability.

The character speaking from the gut shows intuition, courage, visceral emotions such as anger and fear and the breath can be affected by the high stakes of a character.

Finally, the character speaking from the groin centre suggests ambition and passion, desires, presence and being grounded.

Exercise 36: Full combo of gestures and four centres

Practice the work

Now imagine playing each of the four centres of Heart, Head, Gut and Groin with the gesture you have been working on in the speech by Lady Anne, listed.

Richard III

Act 1 Scene 2

Lady Anne:
What, do you tremble? Are you all afraid?
Alas, I blame you not; for you are mortal,
And mortal eyes cannot endure the devil.
Avaunt, thou dreadful minister of hell!
Thou hadst but power over his mortal body:
His soul thou canst not have; therefore begone.
Foul devil, for God's sake, hence, and trouble us not;
For thou hast made the happy earth thy hell,
Fill'd it with cursing cries and deep exclaims.
If thou delight to view thy heinous deeds,
Behold this pattern of thy butcheries.
O gentlemen! See, see dead Henry's wounds
Open their congeal'd mouths and bleed afresh.
Blush, Blush, thou lump of foul deformity,

> For 'tis thy presence that exhales this blood
> From cold and empty veins where no blood dwells:
> Thy deed, inhuman and unnatural
> Provokes this deluge most unnatural.
> O God! Which this blood mad'st, revenge his death;
> O earth! Which this blood drink'st, revenge his death;
> Either heav'n with lightning strike the murderer dead,
> Or earth gape open wide and eat him quick,
> As thou dost swallow up this good King's blood
> Which his hell-govern'd arm hath butchered.

How does it affect the text?

How does it affect the voice?

Does the gesture help support the ideas?

Try the same exercise with other texts that you know, and notice if it clarifies thoughts, breath, feelings that can support your text work further.

In our next chapter we explore stamina which affects the breath, power, volume, and endurance.

Suggested texts

Robert Frost, 'Nothing gold can stay', *Complete Poems of Robert Frost* (2023), New York.

Further reading

Chekhov, M. (1993), *On the Technique of Acting*. Harper Collins Publishers Australia.

Chekhov, M. (2014), *To the Actor, On the Technique of Acting*, New York: Martino Publishing, Harper & Row.

Dixon, G. (2021), *The Master Key to Acting Freedom*, London: MoshPit Publishers.

Rushe, Sinead (2019), *Michael Chekhov's Acting Technique, A Practitioner's Guide*, London: Methuen Drama.

Shakespeare, William (1995), *The Sonnets and A Lovers Complaint*, London: Penguin Classics.
Shakespeare, William (2010), *The Complete Works of Shakespeare: The Arden Shakespeare*, London: Bloomsbury.
Wong, K. K. (1996), *The Complete Book of Tai Chi Chuan: A comprehensive guide to principles and philosophies.* Vermont, NC: Tuttle Publishing.

3 Stamina – Inspired by Tadashi Suzuki

> To maintain success, stamina is more important than talent. You have to learn to be a marathon runner. *JOAN RIVERS*
>
> Imagination is everything, it is the preview of life's coming attractions. *ALBERT EINSTEIN*

Stamina meaning:

1. Sustain physical effort.
2. Secret of their stamina.
3. Endurance.

Introduction

In this chapter we will explore voice and stamina through the great acting methodology of Tadashi Suzuki, who is a leading Japanese director, writer and philosopher, and founder of the Suzuki Company of Toga (SCOT). His style of actor training is very well known across the world, and many companies and artists in the UK and the US have participated in his style of training. He developed a way to train actors known as the Suzuki Method, to build an actor's awareness of the body including the core muscles. It draws on the influences of traditional Japanese and Greek theatre, martial arts and ballet. His principles suggest energy production, breath calibration and centre of gravity control and he utilises a collection of his exercises to disrupt and challenge the actor's breathing and physical and emotional awareness. The 'animal energy' he suggests in his book *Culture is the Body*, resides in the body that produces animal energy rather than manufactured energy.

Although I have adopted and adapted many of the Suzuki exercises over the last twenty years in my voice training for breath and enhanced feet and leg work, I will concentrate in this chapter on a few of his more well-known movements to support voice and stamina, creating a strong body and explore vocal power. I have found that actors in rehearsal cannot always sustain and maintain a physical or vocal energy, due to lack of basic stamina. Having worked in this way myself as a student, and further explored the work on a deeper level as part of my own daily practice which I enhanced further in workshops, online training videos and books, I have found my own stamina is much improved and also that of my students. I do not concentrate solely on consolidating all the core values inherent in Suzuki's work, I take a path that works for me. I know it will also work for my students and hopefully for you too. I also use this work to support physical stamina working through classical text. For me, this works particularly well when I am directing the plays of Shakespeare, the Jacobean and Spanish dramas, and the Greek tragedies. Stamina needs to be maintained and harnessed. Sometimes student actors may struggle with the physical and vocal stamina of these difficult plays, and this daily practice will support them.

Wonderful performances of physical and vocal feats truly are spellbinding, such as Clint Dyer's and Roy Williams' play *Death of England Trilogy*, which required each actor (Thomas Coombes as Michael and Paapa Essiedu as Delroy) to hold the audience each night playing every role each character discusses. A true masterpiece that also covers the accents of all the characters and their physicalities. Further to that, when we watch a great piece of theatre, we should not be aware of the length of thought, or the physical stamina required. When an actor transports us to the place, time and story, it shows the actor is really doing an excellent job in vocally working through the text. If you managed to catch the performance of Kae Tempest's play *Paradise* at the National Theatre, directed by Ian Rickson, you will have seen voice in action, integrated with strong accent and deliberate use of cross-gender acting. The play is a take on Sophocles' mythical play about the war hero, Philoctetes. The actor Lesley Sharp playing Philoctetes, showed remarkable physical and vocal stamina. Kae Tempest and the cast set out to cross-examine the notion of military life and its impact. For those not able to catch this performance, all male characters were written for women to play the male roles as nonbinary. The performances were punchy, aggressive, enthusiastic, authentic and strong, where the stamina and integrity were not in question, nor were the actors sweating the technique, or proving how hard they were working.

A contrast to not sweating the technique would be when you see Olympians being interviewed straight after a race. They are still able to talk, albeit whilst struggling for breath, and you can see how hard their abdominals are working to allow the diaphragm to rise and fall and to manage the lung capacity for speech. Their recovery to be interviewed after such a race is astonishing. However, I wish those interviewers would allow a little more time for recovery so that their thought processes are clearer to communicate, a little more than how happy they are and well they have done! Their lungs have the breath to speak but the mind is still in the race.

Warm-up of toes, feet and legs

Feel the work: Suzuki warm up

This warm-up is necessary before trying any of the Suzuki work as a lot of stress is placed in the legs and injuries can be a common theme if not warmed up correctly. At all times in every exercise maintain a blank expression and allow your imagination to create a fiction of what you are experiencing.

Exercise 1: Toes

Sitting on a chair with your feet flat on the floor spread your toes as far apart as you can. Maintain this hold for 10 seconds.

Repeat this 5 times.

Still seated point the toes upwards and hold for 5 seconds.

Now move the toes towards the right and hold.

Then repeat on the left and hold.

Repeat this 5 times.

Now curl the toes underneath and hold for 5 seconds.

Repeat this 5 times.

Now place a few items by your feet such as a pencil, a small ball, a scrunched-up piece of paper.

Take the items from one foot, using your toes, and place them by the other foot. Repeat this process with the other foot and observe the effort. Notice if this creates tension in any other part of the body, including the face, tongue and jaw.

Understand the work: Toes and feet

The feet contact the floor in several ways. *Notice when you have your shoes on how you walk, can you feel your toes and feet?* Observe walking in socked feet and then bare feet. The relationship to the ground through the feet is key to this stamina work and supports creating a connection to the ground. When you are grounded through the feet you may feel an electrical static on your body which will drain away. This can be known as earthing, as you increase blood flow in your feet and up your body. When you touch the ground with your bare feet the electrons flow through you as the Earth's surface has a supply of mobile electrons that gives the ground we walk on a natural negative electric charge.

Practice the work: Barefoot walking

Practice walking on the ground in bare feet for 20 minutes per day to allow sufficient electrons to transfer to your body.

Exercise 2: Foot rotations for ankles

Standing on one leg rotate the foot and ankle 10 times clockwise and anticlockwise.

Stand on tiptoes and hold for 10 seconds then slowly release the heels down to a flat foot. Repeat this 10 times.

Exercise 3: Wind pose or knee to chest pose

Lie on the floor bringing the right knee up towards the chest and hold it. The left leg can stay long on the floor or bent at the knee. As you breathe out allow the leg to be gently pulled towards your chest and hold it there for 1 minute. Make sure to

Figure 3.1 Wind pose.

release any tension in your shoulders and arms. Gently pulling the knee towards your chest on the outward breath, bring the knee even further towards your chest. Stay in the pose for 1 minute.

Gently and very slowly release the leg to the floor and notice the heat in your hip and groin area and observe how much longer the right leg feels.

Repeat on the left leg.

Understand the work: Wind pose or knee to chest pose

This pose is known as wind pose in yin yoga, but is really a passive stretch exercise. It will open and stretch the fascia and ligaments around the hips, it improves digestion and releases tension in the abdomen, hips and lower back.

Exercise 4: Happy baby pose

Lying down in semi-supine, lift both your legs up so that you can hold your feet, or legs. Create stillness in this pose. Try to

Figure 3.2 Happy baby pose.

relax your shoulders. You should be in a position that suggests a happy baby holding the feet. Hold this position as it releases blood to the hips. Stay there for 1 minute.

Understand the work: Happy baby pose

This pose opens the hips, inner thighs, hamstring and groin, and releases the hips and back.

Exercise 5: Caterpillar pose

From a seated position, with your legs outstretched in front of you, fold forward from the hips, allowing your spine to round. Relax your legs and allow your feet to naturally fall outwards or inwards. Create stillness in this pose. Hold the pose for 5 minutes.

Understand the work: Caterpillar pose

You are looking for sensations along the spine and in the hamstrings and calves. This can also help with digestion as you fold forward as your stomach compresses.

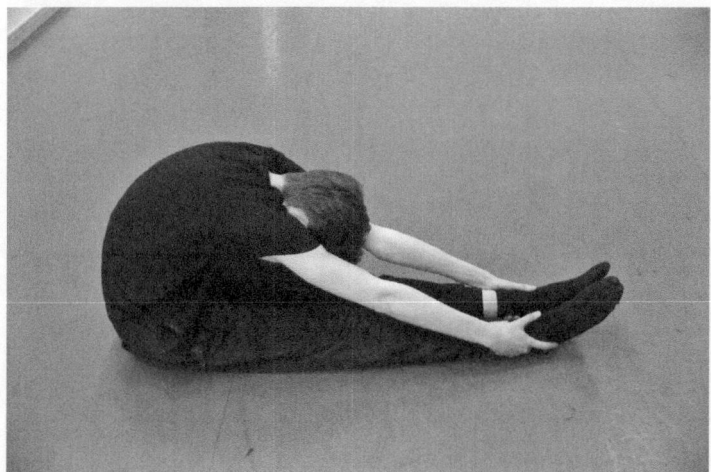

Figure 3.3 Caterpillar pose.

Exercise 6: Dangling pose

Stand with your feet hip-width apart, with your knees slightly bent.

Fold forward allowing your spine to round like a bicycle chain.

Clasp your elbows with opposite hands and create stillness in this pose.

Hold for 2 minutes.

Understand the work: Dangling pose

This pose loosens the hamstrings and warms up the quadriceps, is a good stretch for the lower back, and also strengths the diaphragm. You are looking for sensations along the spine, all the way down from the neck, and a gentle stretch in thighs, hips and the hamstrings.

Squats

Figure 3.4 Squat pose Malasana.

Exercise 7: Squat pose Malasana

This pose stretches the thighs, groin, hips, ankles and torso. It tones the abdomen muscles and increases circulation and blood flow in thighs and pelvis.

Understand the work: Squat pose Malasana

You are looking for sensations along the spine, all the way down from the neck, and a gentle stretch in the thighs and the hamstrings. It tones and strengthens the legs, hips and lower back, enhancing stability in the lower body.

Exercise 8: Moving, in pairs

In pairs, walk slowly around the space, speaking with your partner for a full 2 minutes. Observe each others breathing when speaking.

Remain in pairs and jog around the space, speaking with your partner, for a full 2 minutes, and observe each others breathing and recovery.

Now run outside or run about in a large studio, and speak with a partner, for a full 2 minutes.

Exercise 9: Balance, in pairs

In pairs, take it in turns, where one of you stands still with your legs wide apart, with your eyes closed, and bringing your heels off the floor. Try speaking your text as you stand on tiptoe, your partner will spot you so that you do not fall.

Repeat with the other partner.

Notice if your balance is compromised, or if you are able to do this exercise easily.

Six squats for breath and stamina.

Exercise 10: The Parallel squat

Squat with your legs hip distance apart, try this 3 times and release an audible breath, some suggested sounds are /s/ and /f/.

Exercise 11: Wide-legged (sumo) squat

Squat down into a wide-legged pose, try this 3 times, and release an audible breath such as /s/ and /f/.

Exercise 12: Plie squat

Squatting in plie, try this 3 times and release an audible breath such as a /f/ or /v/.

Exercise 13: Sumo squat on toes

Squat on tiptoes, pointed at a 45-degree angle. Try this 3 times, and release an audible breath, such as /v/.

Exercise 14: Lateral squat

Bring your feet close together and squat low. Try this 3 times and release an audible breath, such as /f/ or /v/.

Exercise 15: Malasana squat

Squatting low down on your haunches, try this 3 times and release an audible breath, such as SH sound.

Understand the work: Squats and breath

Squats and the muscles used provide excellent support of lung function and also strengthens the leg muscles including the calves, quadriceps and hamstrings. To do squats requires the leg muscles to ask the lungs to provide more oxygen, therefore working your heart and lungs. This also strengthens your core muscles, strengthens the muscles of your lower body, boosts athletic abilities, and provides strength and stamina.

Your body should be warmed up and you should feel the breath working hard as it has been exercising the gluteus maximus, minimus and medius (buttocks). You have also been working on the quadriceps (front of the thigh) and the hamstrings (back of the thigh), the groin, hips and calves. Now just stand and breathe. Notice the effort. Notice your recovery.

The focus on toe, foot and leg warm-up and movements helps regulate the breathing and builds stamina and a body ready to work.

Once you have warmed up your leg muscles use a familiar sample of text that you know well, and recognise your breathing and recovery.

Practice the work: Squats

Try speaking the Shakespeare sonnet number 27 whilst in one of the squat poses, and finally with your eyes closed and on tiptoe.

> Weary with toil, I haste me to my bed,
> The dear repose for limbs with travel tired;
> But then begins a journey in my head,
> To work my mind, when body's work's expired:
> For then my thoughts, from far where I abide,
> Intend a zealous pilgrimage to thee,
> And keep my drooping eyelids open wide,
> Looking on darkness which the blind do see:
> Save that my soul's imaginary sight
> Presents thy shadow to my sightless view,
> Which, like a jewel hung in ghastly night,
> Makes black night beauteous and her old face new.
> Lo! Thus, by day my limbs, by night my mind,
> For thee and for myself no quiet find.

(Video)

Exercise 16: The stomp

Start with your socks on, and your feet parallel, with your legs very slightly bent. Your arms are relaxed by your sides, not rigid nor loose. Your hands create a gentle fist, without showing any tension.

Keep the upper body at the same height and eye level throughout, with the core strength activated and the downward direction as mentioned in Chapter 2, where you are fully grounded. Think of the energy in a downward direction connection with the ground.

Next, swing the right leg out fast and then pull in with knee bent as powerfully as you can.

Next, stomp the right leg down very powerfully, immediately adjacent to the left leg.

Then drive your right foot forwards along the floor keeping the same height and eye level, leaving the left leg straight, the heel on the ground and the entire weight on the front of the right leg.

Next stand on tiptoes.

Then bring the legs together

Repeat on the left leg; nothing moves in the upper body only the legs.

Understand the work: The stomp

The actor should stay grounded, when moving or stationary. This individual stomp is the action that most exemplifies the Suzuki Method, because it is the most practical way for an actor to become grounded whilst stationary.

Practice the work: The stomp

Stand with legs and feet together and knees slightly bent or soft.

Bring your right leg up, bent at the knee, to hip height. Use your voice to release a sound such as the HUH sound or try your own sound. Next bring the right leg down, connecting strongly to the earth, and release the sound again.

Repeat with the left leg, using a quick sound of HUH or a sound you prefer.

Repeat the process again keeping the leg raised and holding your balance. Speak some text. Repeat on the left side.

Next make this stomp faster as you move around the space creating a strong upper body and strong legs and feet.

Tips for teachers
You can ask your students to stop at any time on this standing posture with one leg maintaining a strong balance. They can speak any text they know. You can ask them to speak the text very quietly, or using full voice.

Take this strong standing pose and begin to stomp across the room in a straight line. Vocalise the HUH or other sounds created by the group on every stomp.

This is the beginning of the ten Suzuki walks with sound.

Tadashi Suzuki walks into sound and speech

Feel the work: Walks

Exercise 17: Suzuki walks (video)

Keeping the upper body still, strong and energised, allow the legs and core strength to do the work. The feet are the physical energy of the body connected to the earth, hence the very physical lower body warm-up.

Try these ten walks accessing the movement, the breath, the sound and finally your text. There are some sounds suggested on the video.

Walk 1: The stomp and moving

Stomping with your hands by your sides, with gentle soft fists, release a breath exhalation with a sound, such as a voiceless /f/ /s/ sh/ sound.

Now repeat the walk, on each stomp make the sound HUH.

Walk 2: Pidgeon toes

The pidgeon toes walk should have the feet be flat footed, with toes pointed inwards, and with your hands behind your back. With a release of a breath on every step, create a sound such as a voiceless /h/ s/f/ k/ sound.

Now repeat the pidgeon toe walk, on each step make the sound HOO.

Walk 3: Bicycle walk

The bicycle walk should have your hands by your side, with the palms facing outward. Imagine you are riding a unicycle, causing your feet to move upwards and inwards. With a release of a breath, expire on each step and release a voiceless /f/k/s / sound.

Now repeat the bicycle walk, and on each step make the sound HEY.

Walk 4: Side kick

The side kick walk is as it suggests with the legs flaying outwards and the feet loose. With your hands behind your back, with your palms facing outwards, and with breath expiration on each step, create your own voiceless sound, or enjoy the sounds /f/s/sh/.

Now repeat the side kick walk, on each step explore the sound HI.

Walk 5: Tippy-toes tiny steps

On tiptoes, take tiny steps, with hands behind the back and palms facing outwards, with breath expiration such as the voiceless sound /h/f/s/.

Now repeat the tippy-toes walk, and on each step explore the sound HEE.

Walk 6: Crab walk

The crab walk suggests you walk on one side, favouring the right side first, with hands by the side. Release a breath on each step with breath expiration the sounds such as /ft/ s/sh/.

Now repeat the crab side walk. Releasing a sound on each step, explore the sound HA.

Walk 7: The side stomp

The side stomp walk is much like the first stomp. This is to the right-side first, and stomp, with hands by the side, then release the breath on a sigh or the following /f/h/s/.

Now repeat the side stomp walk on the other side, then on each step make the sound HO.

Walk 8: The cross stomp

The cross stomp once again is similar to the other stomps in terms of physical energy through the floor, but the legs cross over each other.

Start with the right side then transfer to the left side going in the opposite direction, across the space. Your hands are by your side, and now release some breath voiceless sounds such /f/s/t/.

Now repeat the cross stomp walk, and on each step make the sound AH.

Walk 9: Kabuki shuffle

The Kabuki shuffle walk allows your feet to be flat on the floor, with your hands by the side. As you shuffle around the space, release a voiceless sound such as /sh/.

Now repeat the Kabuki shuffle walk, and on each step make the sound sustained SSHHHHHH.

Walk 10: Cockroach shuffle

The cockroach shuffle walk allows you to shuffle on tiptoes with the knees bent. Your arms are bent at the elbows with your palms facing upwards, as if carrying a tray. Now release a voiceless sound such as /ft/h/.

Now repeat the cockroach shuffle walk, and on each step make the sound EE.

Now flop to the floor and feel your breath, stretch out your legs and take some water.

Understand the work: Ten walks

The purpose of these walks is to challenge the actors' control and awareness of the body's centre of gravity, by suggesting physical problems they must confront: being aware of the self, remain focused at all times, keep an expressionless face. Also to separate the lower body from the upper body to create freer movement and breath support.

Statues sitting and standing

Exercise 18: Statues: low, mid and upper pose (video)

Low pose statues

Stand in a neutral position. Now crouch low, with your feet apart (as low as some of the squats). The energy should feel low and release a breath.

Next release a sound in crouch low pose position.

Finally, release some text in low pose position.

Now repeat the exercises of low pose position and create a statue and speak your text.

Mid pose statue

From standing in a neutral position, crouch to a mid level with your feet apart, than lower yourself quickly down into a mid position statue. The energy should feel low but ready for action, and release a breath.

Next release a sound in mid pose statue.

Finally, release some text in mid pose statue.

Now repeat the exercises of mid crouch position and create a statue and speak your text.

Tiptoes upper pose statue

From standing in a neutral position, with your feet apart, raise yourself up quickly into a tiptoe statue. The energy should feel up and high, and release a breath.

Next release a sound in tiptoes statue position.

Finally, release some text in tiptoe position.

Now repeat the exercises of tiptoe pose and create a statue and speak your text.

Practice the work: The full combo of statues

The statues can be distinct at each level, each time you try them, high, low, or medium or mid, but it is important to emphasise the whole body is engaged facing forward.

Create three poses again in low pose, middle pose and high pose levels. High pose should be done on tiptoes, or at least with your heels off the floor.

In each of the statue poses speak some text. Try it first in a quiet voice, then in full volume. *What do you observe of yourself in the work?*

Tips for teachers

You can try the exercises over and over and perhaps create this as a warm-up for a rehearsal. Try the same exercises again adding the following short sounds:

> Low pose statue position, make the FT sound like a bow and arrow.
>
> Mid pose statue position, make the sound SH like a shower.
>
> High pose statue position, make the sound HA like you are surprised.

Switch quite quickly between each one to build stamina in the body with immediate responses in quick succession.

Now try the same crouch poses again sounding through intoning the following:

> Low pose statue with the sound AH.
>
> Mid pose statue with the sound OH.
>
> High pose statue with the sound EE.

What do you observe of yourself in the work?

Exercise 19: Sitting poses on the floor

The rest pose requires you to sit on the floor in tucked ball, with your arms hugging your knees. Stillness should be maintained. This is a resting pose before the sitting poses begin and which you can come back to, in order to regain your breath.

Sitting pose 1: balance on your sitting bones, arms and legs in ball, and your feet on the floor. Maintain stillness and breathe.

Sitting pose 2: stretch your legs out in front, with your arms out in front. Stillness should be maintained if possible and breathe.

Sitting pose 3: stretch your legs out with an open wide stance, and your arms should also stretch out wide. Stillness should be maintained and breathe.

Now move between the sitting poses of 1, 2 and 3 and back to seated rest pose, the tucked ball position, each time adopting a different breath quality or voiceless sound. Some examples suggested: fff/sh/zzz/vvv/.

Now try the same sitting poses again switching between each pose, sounding the following:

Sitting pose 1: intone the sound HEE.

Sitting pose 2: intone the sound HO.

Sitting pose 3: intone the sound HA.

Now in each of the sitting poses speak your text offering distinct ways of delivery.

Use your text to speak quietly/softly as if alone.

Next speak your text as if you are desperate for someone near you to hear.

Finally, use your text on full voice, with volume that may carry across a large space.

What happens to your voice in each of the positions?

Understand the work: Sitting and standing

The standing and sitting statues work on core strength, challenge stillness, stability, the stamina and the resilience, and the ability to maintain good breath control.

Exercise 20: Calls, shouts and statues

Standing in neutral, raise the soft palate and yawn.

Feel the stretch at the back of the mouth and repeat several times. The mouth is open as in 'hot'. This will create what Arthur Lessac calls the inverted megaphone.

Sounding the list of words below, take one hand away from your mouth as if you see the words flying across the room. Allow your arm to travel with the word allowing the sound to move across the room. Let the length of the vowel hit the furthest wall.

Hey

Hee

Hi

Ho

hoo

Now, in pairs, be as far away from your partner as possible in the space. Using the statues of high, mid and low explore the voice projected across the space exploring the list of sentences:

Hello, how are you?

I won the championship!

Can you come here?

I can't believe it!

Let us celebrate.

Understand the work

Once you begin a call, it can lead to an extended sound of intoning which can help the sound carry across the space, creating a safe way to call and shout. You are using the opening of the mouth like a megaphone to imagine the sound flowing across the space. Keep the mouth open in the megaphone shape for all calls and shouts.

Try the text listed, using sitting and standing statue poses, and using extended volume and power. This text is from Shakespeare's *Richard III* which allows you to draw on an extensive vocal range, to playing with power and volume whilst accessing the stamina and physicality to play this role. I have suggested some sitting and standing poses, but you may equally choose your own.

Richard III

Act 1 Scene 4

Duke of Clarence:

(*sitting rest pose*)

O, I have pass'd a miserable night,
So full of ugly sights, of ghastly dreams,

(*sitting pose 1*)

That, as I am a Christian faithful man,
I would not spend another such a night
Though 'twere to buy a world of happy days,
So full of dismal terror was the time!

(*sitting pose 2*)

Methoughts that I had broken from the Tower,
And was embark'd to cross to Burgundy;
And in my company my brother Gloucester,
Who from my cabin tempted me to walk
Upon the hatches: thence we look'd toward England,
And cited up a thousand fearful times,

(*low pose statue*)

During the wars of York and Lancaster,
That had befall'n us. As we paced along
Upon the giddy footing of the hatches,
Methought that Gloucester stumbled, and in falling,
Struck me (that thought to stay him) overboard,
Into the tumbling billows of the main.

(high pose statue)

O Lord! Methought, what pain it was to drown:
What dreadful noise of waters in mine ears;
What ugly sights of death within mine eyes!

(mid pose statue)

Methought, I saw a thousand fearful wrecks;
Ten thousand men that fishes gnaw'd upon;
Wedges of gold, great anchors, heaps of pearl,
Inestimable stones, unvalu'd jewels,

(low pose statue)

All scatter'd in the bottom of the sea.
Some lay in dead men's skulls; and, in those holes
Where eyes did once inhabit, there were crept –
As 'twere in scorn of eyes – reflecting gems,
Which woo'd the slimy bottom of the deep,
And mock'd the dead bones that lay scatter'd by.

Cool-down body scan

Exercise 20: Cool-down walking meditation

This walking meditation is also designed as a cool-down. Conscious walking supports true connection to feet, legs and breath. It is mindful and reflective. This is a helpful way to connect back to the toes and feet after the squats and walking and sitting statues done earlier.

Slowly lift one foot and gently place it down in front of the other foot, consciously moving from heel to ball of foot to toe each time. Observe your weight and balance from one foot to the other. Shift your weight into ball and then the toes. Make sure the journey is one of complete sacrifice to the commitment of engaging with most of the foot. Think heel, ball, toe, then slowly lift the heel of the other foot. Observe your breath.

Practice the work: Walking meditation practice for 5 minutes

Finally, find your way to lying down, and re-explore the wind pose, the happy baby pose and the caterpillar pose once more to stretch out your leg, calf, hamstrings and gluteus muscles. The release of lactic acid during the intensive workout breaks once stretching is back in the muscles. This allows for repair and recovery and improves circulation.

Suggested texts

Laurence Dunbar, 'Keep A-pluggin' Away', *Selected Poems* (2004), London: Penguin Classics.
Alice Cary, 'Perseverance'. *Collection of Alice and Pheobe Cary* (2016), California: Create Space Independant Publishers Platform.
Rudyard Kipling, 'If', *Selected Poems* (2004), London: Penguin Classics.

Further reading

Allain, Paul (2009), *The Theatre Practice of Tadashi Suzuki*, London: Bloomsbury Methuen Drama.
Cleather, D. (2018), *The Little Black Book of Training Wisdom: How to train and improve any sport*, CreateSpace Independant Publishing Platform, UK.
Suzuki, T. (1990), *The Way of Acting. Theatre Communications Group*. London: Nick Hern Books.
Suzuki, T. (2015), *Culture is the Body. Theatre Communications Group*, London: Nick Hern Books.
Oida, Yoshi and Marshall, Lorna (1997), *The Invisible Actor*, London: Methuen.
Shakespeare, William (1995), *The Sonnets and A Lovers Complaint*, London: Penguin Classics.

Shakespeare, William (2010), *The Complete Works of Shakespeare: The Arden Shakespeare*, London: Bloomsbury.

Tempest, K. (2021), *Paradise*, Picador, UK.

Williams, R. and Dyer, C. (2020), *Death of England*. (Delroy), Methuen Drama, UK.

Williams, R. and Dyer C. (2020), *Death of England*. (Michael), Methuen Drama, UK.

4 Pitch and Pace – 'Viewpoints' Inspired

Tone has the living soul. *SHINICHI SUZUKI*

10% of conflict is due to a difference of opinion. 90% is due to the wrong tone of voice. *FRANCOIS DE LA ROCHEFOUCAULD*

Tone meaning:

1. They were tuned into my way of thinking.
2. Her tone rose steadily in pitch.
3. A state in which people agree or understand each other.
4. Concur or harmony.

Introduction

In this chapter we will explore how voice training can be re-imagined through the body, and in space, time and gestures, creating voice exercises using the work of Mary Overlie's six viewpoints and also the work of Anne Bogart and Tina Landau, through what they term as the nine 'Viewpoints'. As a voice teacher I employ 'Viewpoints' to explore pitch and pace within text, I also adopt this method when directing in regard to space and shape, to explore the dynamics in voice training by further securing the interconnectedness across voice, movement and acting. This work can be helpful to some student actors, where they may struggle with other methods of acting or movement practitioners.

While 'Viewpoints', a technique of dance composition, has been part of the dance tradition that the choreographer Mary Overlie first coined to refer to the six elements of space, story, time, shape, movement and emotion, it gives further scope to the idea that voice training does not work in isolation.

The best-known practitioners of 'Viewpoints' are Anne Bogart and Tina Landau who used the approach to develop movement, training actors and building ensemble. Bogart and Overlie both taught in the late 1970s at New York University's Experimental Theatre Wing, and Bogart was inspired by her colleague Overlie to work as an actor and director. Tina Landau, the American playwright and director, collaborated with Bogart over the following decade expanding the original work set out by Overlie. Later Bogart co-founded the theatre company Saratoga International Theatre Institute (SITI) with director Tadashi Suzuki in 1992 which we have already explored in Chapter 3.

Warm-up the five senses

Exercise 1: Warm-up: the senses

Take 30 seconds to notice what you see, in the space you are in. Try not to over think this exercise.

Sense 1: Sight

Now close your eyes and cover your eyes further with your hands. Stay in the warmth and darkness of your hands for 1 minute. Notice your breathing in this exercise.

Now take your hands away and open your eyes.

What do you see with fresh eyes? Are the colours clearer or brighter?

Do you notice something you had not observed before?

Release a breath.

Release the sustained sound AH.

Sense 2: Sound
Now listen to what is going on around you.

Next, stop up your ears with your middle finger and lightly tap on the middle finger another finger on the same hand creating a drumming rhythmic quality. Do this for approximately 2 minutes.

Now take your hands away from your ears.

What do you notice? What can you hear with fresh ears?

Release a breath.

Release the sustained sound OH.

Sense 3: Smell
Now breathe in through the nose and out through the mouth.

What do you smell? What do you notice about the air or the feeling as air enters your lungs?

Now stop up both nostrils so that you must breathe through the mouth.

Now take the hands away from the nose and take a big breath in through the nose.

Is the air you can smell, the cooking of something? The sweat of something?

Release a sigh on the outward breath.

Now release the sustained sound MMMMM.

Sense 4: Taste
Now roll your tongue around your mouth and notice the teeth, the gums, your tongue. Swallow a few times and notice your breath.

Release a breath or a sigh.

Release a sustained sound of YUM.

Sense 5: Touch

Finally, find something to touch that is yours. It may be something in your bag. Feel the fabric, the bag, really enjoy the sensation with touch. Then try the same with your eyes closed and notice how physical sensations make you appreciate the texture of the thing you are holding.

Release a breath or a sigh.

Release on a sustained sound of OO.

Does this exercise conjure up images or memories, thoughts or feelings?

Exercise 2: Space, colours and observation

In the room or studio you are in, notice all the colours and textures.

Find all the things that are green, and loudly express the sentence 'I found green' as many times as you can.

Find all the things that are blue, and loudly express the sentence 'I found blue' as many times as you can.

Find the things that are yellow, and loudly express the sentence 'I found yellow' as many times as you can.

Find the things that are red, and loudly express the sentence 'I found red' as many times as you can.

Find the things that are white, purple, black, grey, and even patterned as many times as you can.

In your studio or room, notice the air, the light, the sounds, the physical sensations, understanding that you are arriving at a place of work that enlivens the imagination. Imagine you are not in any room, but the room that offers something to you today.

You may find that text opens itself to you more as you are seeing, hearing and feeling your senses come alive.

Speak the Shakespeare sonnet listed with a new appreciation of your five senses. See it, smell it, hear it, touch it and taste it.

> Sonnet 8
>
> Music to hear, why hear'st thou music sadly?
> Sweets with sweets war not, joy delights in joy;

Why lov'st thou that which thou receiv'st not gladly,
Or else receives'st with pleasure thine annoy?
If the true concord of well-tuned sounds,
By unions married, do offend thine ear,
They do but sweetly chide thee, who confounds
In singleness the parts that thou shouldst bear.
Mark how one string, sweet husband to another,
Strikes each in each by mutual ordering;
Resembling sire, and child, and happy mother,
Who, all in one, one pleasing note do sing;
Whose speechless song, being many, seeming one,
Sings this to thee: 'thou single wilt prove none'.

Understand the work: The senses

Using the five senses to appreciate where you are and recognise being truly present is an effective way to start the work. The senses of sight, hearing, taste, touch and smell makes us human. There are two other senses less well known. Sense six is proprioception which allows humans to keep track of where our body parts move and coordinate in space, and sense seven is the vestibular, which means to maintain balance and gravity for movement.

'Viewpoints' of space, shape, gesture, tempo and topography

Feel the work: Space (distance between you and others or things on stage)

Exercise 3

Move around the space/studio or room you are in, and move away from or towards a wall, a door or a window. Below are a list of words to explore your relationship to space and how it affects pitch.

Walk towards the wall or door or window expressing the words listed.

Far

Near

Up

Down

Forward

Back

Dark

Bright

In

Out

Left

Right

Diagonal

Ask yourself the following questions.

What happens if I move close to the wall, window or door?

What happens to the words or intentions if I move away from the wall, window or door?

How does it affect the pitch of a word or the pace?

Exercise 4: Text and space

Get remarkably close to a wall and say the sentences listed ten times. Notice how you feel, notice if the pitch is higher or lower. Also observe how differently you feel each time you move closer to or away from the wall.

Sentence 1. 'What a beautiful day' then take a step back, then say it again. Keep repeating the line until it feels the most comfortable way to speak the line. Notice how near or far you are to the wall, and how it affects pitch.

Now say the following sentences ten times, and each time take a step backwards and then a step forward.

Sentence 2. 'I feel very uncomfortable' take a step back. Now say the line again stepping forward. *Can you sense the change in pitch change?*

Sentence 3. 'I want to tell you something important' take a step back, then repeat the line taking a step forward. Notice if the pitch changes here too.

Sentence 4. 'I like your bike' take a step back, then take a step forward, and say the line again.

Once again, have you noticed if the pitch changes depending on the sentence or the distance?

Sentence 5. 'I'll be fine' take a step back, then say the line again, and take a step forward.

What does it do to the text? Does the space either near or far affect the line?

So far, these sentences have been done to a wall, door or window.

Exercise 5: In pairs (space)

What happens if you now collaborate with a partner?

Repeat the previous lines to a partner. Start off close to each other. Say a sentence each. Move forward or back noticing the space between you.

What do you notice about how each line makes you feel? How does it make your partner feel? Is the space too close? Are there any of the lines that could be said very closer to your partner? Or do you feel you ought to be further away? What does the pitch do in each of the sentences?

Now try the same exercise moving further and further away from the person. Observe the impact each of those lines has on you and the other person.

Understand the work: Space

The distance between people or things on stage affects pitch and pace, it can also affect volume and intentions. Space is imperative as a decision for actors. By exploring spatial awareness in relation to others, or stage furniture, or props, we can understand the interconnectedness between space, pitch and pace. Getting too close to someone creates tension, affects the breath, asks you, the actor to consider pitch and how does that affect all the other characters? Is it appropriate to the scene? Spatial awareness is knowing where your body is in relation to objects or people. To understand the right choice of spatial awareness, you also need to understand and respond to a change in position from these objects or people.

When we are speaking to a stranger, we tend to place ourselves at a polite distance that we can converse more comfortably. That would be around a metre away, and yet when the distance of space is broken, either too large or too small, it can, for example, make us feel uncomfortable, intimidated, or attracted to the other person.

The characters that you play may have different approaches to space than you. Unfamiliar cultural backgrounds need to be observed.

Imagine if a fellow actor comes close to you to as they speak. What do you think the audience understands from that spatial closeness? What happens to you in everyday social life? Do you lean back?

A polite distance depends on circumstances of course, with the countryside and rural areas vastly different from a city, or another way to put it is the urban versus rural context. Circumstances of proximity such as on a crowded train are considered ok, as it represents the context. But less appropriate if you are somewhere else such as a doctor's waiting room for example. The context of space matters. If the character you are playing is wealthy and has status, then consider the more personal space you may feel you own. Or the poorer your character is, the less space you may want to occupy.

Each one is a choice, and in which case, how does it affect pitch?

Practice the work: Space, in pairs
Exercise 6

In pairs using the sentences listed, move towards or away from each other and notice the story you are telling considering the spatial awareness, and the pitch and pace, and notice the impact each line your character says and how it affects the scene.

Sentence 1. 'I do not like you when you are like this.'

Sentence 2. 'I am not happy either.'

Sentence 3. 'I want to discuss the situation.'

Sentence 4. 'I need to take some time to think.'

Sentence 5. 'Drink this.'

Sentence 6. 'No, I don't want to.'

Sentence 7. 'Yes, for me.'

Sentence 8. 'You're funny.'

Sentence 9. 'You are too.'

Exercise 7: Practice further: solo and space

Next, using the poem listed, try the space exercise delivering the lines to the wall again. Try different qualities of volume and pitch and notice when you have the impulse to move back or forward creating distance or closeness.

Poem

I walk towards you, expecting a response.
Do not walk away.

What can I expect this time?
When I gave you the gift of life.
You've changed since I last saw you, and,
so have I,
but we should still remain together.
you and I.
Will you rise in the sky, like the breath of fresh air?
Or fly, like a bird, in the gentle breeze?
Although you are gone, you are still here,
I see you everywhere, in the flowers and in the trees.
But come to me, when I too shall fly,
And we, are together as one, when I shall die.

Practice the work further: Solo space

Using text you are familiar with, move towards or away from the wall, door or window, allowing you the actor to comprehend and make choices of how we all interpret space. Feeling the benefit of spatial awareness between characters explores the dynamics of individuals, and how it affects and reflects the characters within a scene. Try it further with text you know very well and speak close to someone, or further away.

What does it do to your scene or monologue? Does it affect the volume? Does it impact on the feelings in the scene?

Notice and observe others and their potential subtext with a clearer understanding of spatial awareness, and the choices you can make as an actor.

Practice the work (in pairs)

With your scene partner using prepared duologues, explore the near and far of space. Also explore the furniture and how you navigate it as you work through your scene. Notice the pitch and pace.

Tips for teachers
You could have half the class watch this exercise, as they get to watch the space of near and far and also navigate the furniture and its relationship to the actors on stage. Perhaps allow your students to feedback what they observe in terms of space, pitch and pace.

Shape

Exercise 8: Shape (lines, curves, sharp edges of the body to create shapes)

Exploring shapes allows the actor to embody a physical presence or space on stage.

Feel the work: Shape

Explore the list of words and try embodying the shape of the word. Try to explore the whole body to find the shape, with your body, your hands, legs, spine, and speak the words as you embody the words.

- Bendy
- Sharp
- Long
- Bulgy
- Pointy
- Jagged
- Round
- Square
- Straight
- Curved.

How does it affect pitch?
How does it affect pace?

Feel the work: Shape of stock characters
Exercise 9

Have a chair close by and either sit or stand in each of the following characters' physicality listed below. These characters can be generalised.

Character shape 1
Elderly 80-year-old person, with limited movement to stand and sit.

Release a breath and notice the energy.

Next release a sound of OH.

What do you notice about their shape? What do you notice about the sounds you might make as you inhabit this character's shape?

Character shape 2
A young 14-year-old teenager, with a range of movements that might be compromised by social settings.

Release a breath and notice this.

Now release the sound OH.

What do you notice about the sounds you might make as you inhabit this character's shape?

Character shape 3
A young child of 5 years old. With the openness and flexibility as they sit or try to stand.

Release a breath and notice the energy.

Now release the sound OH.

What do you notice about the sounds you might make as you inhabit this character's shape?

Practice the work: Stock characters' shapes

Take one of the three stock characters you explored earlier, allow them to sit and stand. Observe more critically the breath, the movement, the sound and finally the sentences listed.

> I am free to do what I want any old time.
> I love drinking coffee.
> I like licking ice-cream.
> My favourite cake is chocolate cake.
> I can blow up a balloon.
> The dog fell into the hole.
> I like dancing to happy music.
> Slow music makes me sad.
> I am bored.
> I have no energy.

Exercise 10

Next explore the other two stock character shapes, using the same sentences.

Did you notice the how the shape affects the pitch, tune, pace or tone of the line?

Understand the work: Shape

Do you have a pose in your everyday life? If so, what is it? Do you stand in a particular way that your friends and family would instantly recognise you from a distance? Is it the way you sit? Notice this about yourself.

Everyone has shapes or poses that they use or are more comfortable with. They are known as muscle motor holds, or muscle motor control. In 'Viewpoints' the movement methodology is known as shapes. Character shapes, the shapes that characters make, tell us who they are. Changing the shape can affect the several aspects of the character's personality, their pitch and their volume. They will have different motor holds for different situations, times of day and emotional states. These are the shapes they will return to most often.

Practice the work further: Shape

Exercise 11

Create the shape of – 'I feel unwell', release a breath, then say the line.

Create the shape of – 'I am in charge', release a breath, then say the line.

Create the shape of – 'I am so happy', release a breath, then say the line.

Create the shape of – 'I am so angry', release a breath, then say the line.

Create the shape of – 'I am in love', release a breath, then say the line.

Create the shape of – 'I'm running away', release a breath, then say the line.

Create the shape of – 'I feel sad', release a breath, then say the line.

Once you have embodied the shape, practice the line that best matches how you feel.

Exercise 12: Changing the shape

Now deliberately change the sentence to a different shape.

Notice if you become quiet on a particular sentence, or you become louder.

How does the line affect speed? Does it affect the shape and the shape affect the line? What does the shape do to the intention? The character? The emotional state? The pitch, tune and the pace?

Gestures: Feel the work (behavioural and expressive gestures are shapes)

Exercise 13

Using the list of words, enjoy playing with each of the gestures, and notice if this affects pitch or tone.

> Point.
>
> Thumb up.
>
> Thumb down.
>
> Punch the air.
>
> Wag the finger.
>
> Wave hello.
>
> Wave goodbye.

Has each word affected the pitch of each gesture?

Exercise 14: Gesture and sound

Now try each of the previous physical gestures using the sound AH HA.

Nod your head up and down – say AH HA.

Nod your head side to side – say AH HA.

Put one hand slowly to your head – say AH HA.

Put both hands quickly to your head – say AH HA.

Now repeat the gesture with the following words.

> Nod your head up and down and say 'yes'.
>
> Nod your head side to side and say 'no'.

Put one hand slowly to your head and say, 'I am sorry.'

Put both hands quickly to your head and say, 'I forgot.'

Give a thumbs up sign and say 'good'.

Give the two thumbs up sign, smile and say 'excellent'.

Now give a thumbs down sign and say 'bad'.

Notice how your voice changes and the enthusiasm and pitch rise or fall for each gesture as the feeling gets stronger.

These are examples of typical united gestures that cuts across cultures, and we are all clear on the meaning.

Practice the work: Gestures

Nod your head up and down and say the word 'yes'.

Nod your head from side to side and say the word 'no'.

Put your hand slowly to your head and say, 'I'm sorry'.

Put your hand quickly to your head and say, 'I forgot'.

Remind yourself to observe the pitch.

Exercise 15: Gesture, in pairs

In pairs, separate out in the room and label yourself (A) and (B).

(A) gestures to (B) 'Do you want a drink?', speaking the line quietly.

Although B understands the gesture, they pretend not to hear by cupping the ear (another gesture).

(A) must repeat the gesture 'Do you want a drink?'. Notice if your pitch and volume rise to convey the meaning to support the gesture. You may become more animated in your face and body to convey your message. The inner breath and outer movement affect gesture and intention.

Practice the work: Gesture

Here are some further sentences to physicalise and notice your pitch, shape and tempo.

What time is it?

I will phone you.

Can I have the bill?

I have not got a clue.

Go away.

I am bored.

Now try some other gestures and speaking the line at the same time.

Understand the work: Gesture

Movements that involve a part or parts of the body, e.g. hands, arms, legs, head, eyes, shoulders, etc., anything that can be isolated to create meaning, convey thoughts and ideas, which affect pitch, pace and speech and breath in a micro way.

Behavioural gestures can be the shrug of the shoulders, the thrust of a hip, for example, or they can convey information of a thought, or an intention. These are more physical, requiring more breath and depth of sound, which can be conscious or unconscious.

Expressive gestures show an internal feeling or emotion: I feel.

Behavioural gestures would suggest an action: I do.

Some incredibly detailed gestures are particular to a character or social context. For example, the tic tac gestures used by bookmakers, now replaced by mobile technology. Croupiers in casinos have gestures, to indicate to their managers certain bets. Gestures are used to get attention to check something. Gestures are used by stock traders, army, and military on recognisance, for example. These gestures can be particular to a character, culture, background, time of day or year, the historical, economic or social context.

There are also gestures that relate mood, such as the palm facing downward with pinkie finger and thumb rocking back and forth, suggests I am ok, or it's ok. There are public and private gestures, gestures that unite us, such as lifting your arms upward to give thanks for winning the football, or your head in your hands to show we have lost the football!

Notice the gestures people use both behavioural and expressive in everyday life. Observe how often you may use a gesture.

Tips for teachers
You can take this session of repeated lines and gestures to extremes, creating a class that allows a student to speak one line of text and use it repeatedly. The group repeats the line and gesture back to the first student. They can make the gesture as big and the sound as creative as they like. This allows the group to support the student as they create either an external expression or internal expression of sound with repeated gestures and lines. Of course, always be mindful that some kinds of gestures are not acceptable or appropriate unless related to specific text.

Feel the work: Tempo (speed, length, response, regularity)

Exercise 16

Using the list of words suggested, explore both the physicality and vocal quality of each word, and how the pitch may be affected by tempo.

- Fast
- Slow
- Rapid
- Quickly
- Brisk

Hurry

Leisurely

Sluggish

Plod.

Try speaking some pre-learned text extremely fast and notice your inner breath and tempo and outer movements.

Now speak the same text slow, again notice your inner breath and tempo and outer movements and tempo.

Now speak your text both fast on some lines and slow on other lines.

How does this affect your inner breath and tempo and outer movements?

What does this do to the overall text? Does it change the meaning or heighten the text?

Now speak the text in slow motion. How does this affect your inner breath and tempo and outer movements?

Then slowly increase the speed.

How does this affect your inner tempo and outer movements?

Practice the work: Tempo

In pairs, using a duologue of your choice, one of you speak extremely fast and the other partner speak slow with care and deliberation.

What does this do to the text and scene?

Some splendid examples of playing with tempo and text are the following:

Glengarry glen ross by David Mamet.

Speed the plough by David Mamet.

Top girls by Carol Churchill.

Much Ado About Nothing by William Shakespeare.

Understand the work: Tempo

Tempo can be evenly paced, fast, slow, upbeat, or deliberately measured to create a mood or feeling in a scene. We do this all the time in speech without thinking. If your character is slow and measured and in a scene which is extremely fast and full of energy, the impact on the character can seem greater.

For example, imagine your character is from a small rural village, and you walk slowly into a café, slowly sit down and order a coffee. Then a fight breaks out on the next table creating fast and furious energy. This could impact your character's tempo for a few seconds until the measured and slow pace returns.

Alternatively, you walk slowly into the café, sit down and order a coffee. Then the fast fight ensues and this time it affects you so that you get up, speak fast and try to calm the situation, or hide, or call the police with frenetic energy. Your energy can impact the scene. Slow action on stage followed by something fast and furious such as movement or music can alter the perception for the audience. Tempo can also affect accent, such as the rate at which we speak. The general school of thought is that those with more space and time will speak more slowly, whereas those that live in a built up fast paced city are more likely to speak faster than their rural counterparts.

Comedians establish a tempo a lot – for the punchline. They will also use it in non-verbal communication such as slapstick. Think Laurel and Hardy, or the Neil Simon films and *The Sunshine Boys*. Writers will use tempo in plays for comedic effect too. The character's tempo will often vary, as does our own. Situations or circumstances within a play can briefly alter that; for example the dropping of a plate, or the noise of a car backfiring, will create a kinaesthetic response, one that is fast and immediate and in the moment. But quickly the energy returns to our natural baseline, depending on the circumstances of course. The character's inner tempo and outer tempo is often through heart and breath. The character's outer tempo is through speed of their movements.

Due to human nature, actors may unintentionally match each other's tempo, but usually different characters have different tempos. They may start a scene with their own tempos but external factors such as a loud noise or a shooting would indicate a shift so that actors are working in the same tempo. A character can mess with all other characters' tempo. Tempo affects how long a character will take to process information, change thoughts and react to something new.

Think about how the police, or mental health professionals are all trained to take the heat out of a situation by speaking slowly and calmly to defuse a difficult encounter.

What happens if you use a measured even tempo in a scene and then shift to a new tempo? How does it affect your inner breath and tempo and outer movement into voice and speech?

Practice the work: Tempo, in pairs

In pairs, or small groups, work on a duologue or scene of your choice.

First speak the scene listening to each other.

Now try one of you being evenly measured in tempo, trying to listen whilst your partner speaks amazingly fast (excited perhaps), even overlapping the dialogue and talking over the top of your partner.

What does this do to the scene?

Now try the scene where both of you are trying to speed up and talk over the top of each other like you are interrupting.

What does this do to the scene?

Finally try the scene where you are both very calm and measured.

How is the scene affected by the tempo you have imposed?

Tips for teachers

You could get your students to eat, drink or chew, fast or slowly, whilst doing the scene, which will affect tempo.

A further exercise is an activity using a monologue, to take everything out of a bag fast, and notice the speed and tempo of the text. Then put everything back slow, calm and measured. Then try the same exercises again only this time take everything out very slowly and measured, then put everything back in the bag amazingly fast, each time speaking the text, and notice how the tempo affects the pitch. The activity helps create a moment of focus and the only task is to speak fast or slow. This also affects inner breath tempo and outer breath tempo and movement.

Feel the work: Topography, creating patterns of movement

Exercise 17

Enter a variety of spaces listed and notice how each one makes you feel. Notice the breath and notice your physicality.

- Cathedral
- Funeral home
- The top of a tall building
- Theatre
- Elevator

Now speak your text as if from each of these spaces. Notice your movement, notice the shapes you make in the space.

What do you observe? How does each place affect your breath, pitch and pace?

Exercise 18

In pairs, tell a simple story to your partner. Your partner will observe how you told the story with your hands, head, shoulders, even eyes. *How do you tell stories with your body patterns in space?*

Your partner will try and remember all the details of your story and the use of your body to mimic some of your gestures, the movement in space and the shapes you may make.

Notice the gestures you use in everyday life; do you use large gestures?

Do you use straight lines, curves, the way you move your arms, hands, head, etc.?

Now try a monologue, noticing the body movements of the character as they tell a story in their monologue.

What can you observe? Are they your gestures and body patterns?

Or are they the gestures that are more appropriate to the character?

Do you sit or stand in the same space as your character? Notice the levels between yourself and the furniture, how high is the ceiling? How does the room affect pitch, pace and volume?

Notice if you make the same patterns in space.

Exercise 19

Finally, imagine you enter a vast space such as a cathedral and you will create a work of art on the wall. Using sounds, not words, create a picture using pitch and sounds and explore the element of patterns in space as you create your masterpiece. Use the large canvas to explore patterns in the space.

Understand the work: Topography

Recognising patterns in space that you do every day helps you notice and understand the shapes and patterns in space that your character might have. Observe how different they are from you. If you are playing a character that has deep rooted psychological issues, their topography patterns in space will be different from your own. This will affect the pitch, pace, breath and stress patterns of a character.

Practice the work: 'Viewpoints' full combo

Using the text listed, from the speech by Lady Anne, working through space, tempo, gestures and or patterns or shapes, observe how this supports pitch and pace and supports further work on acting and voice through viewpoints.

Richard III

Act 1 Scene 2

Lady Anne:

Set down, set down your honourable load,
If honour may be shrouded in a hearse,
Whilst I awhile obsequiously lament
The untimely fall of virtuous Lancaster.
Poor key-cold figure of a holy king!
Pale ashes of the house of Lancaster!
Thou bloodless remnant of that royal blood!
Be it lawful that I invocate thy ghost,
To hear the lamentations of Poor Anne,
Wife to thy Edward, to thy slaughter'd son,
Stabb'd by the self same hand that made these wounds!
Lo, in these windows that let forth thy life,
I pour the helpless balm of my poor eyes.
Cursed be the hand that made these fatal holes!
Cursed be the heart that had the heart to do it!
Cursed the blood that let this blood from hence!
More direful hap betide that hated wretch,
That makes us wretched by the death of thee,
Than I can wish to adders, spiders, toads,
Or any creeping venom'd thing that lives!
If ever he have child, abortive be it,
Prodigious, and untimely brought to light,
Whose ugly and unnatural aspect

May fright the hopeful mother at the view;
And that be heir to his unhappiness!
If ever he have wife, let her be made
A miserable by the death of him
As I am made by my poor lord and thee!
Come, now towards Chertsey with your holy load,
Taken from Paul's to be interred there;
And still, as you are weary of the weight,
Rest you, whiles I lament King Henry's corpse.

Tips for teachers
When students get stuck on a thought or an idea, this work can help unlock the thoughts and intentions as the actors work through the body. Splitting the group into two halves so that there is an observation of the work can be hugely beneficial. Allow time to observe the viewpoints through pitch and pace, and develop observation, critical evaluation of a process and what might need further refining.

Suggested texts

Priya Yanambaka, *The Topography of Your Body* (2016), Woodstock, CA: PoetrySoup.
Carol Churchill, *Top Girls* (1984), London: Methuen Drama.
David Mamet, *Glengarry Glen Ross* (1984), New York: Methuen Drama US.
William Shakespeare, *Much Ado About Nothing* (2016), London: Arden.

Further reading

Bogart, A. and Landau, T. (2014) *The Viewpoints Book; A practical guide to viewpoints and composition*, London: Nick Hern Books.
Carey, D. and Carey Clark, R. (2008), *Vocal Arts Workbook* and DVD, London: Methuen Drama.
Robison, K. (2000), *The Actor Sings*, Portsmouth: Heinemann.
Rodenberg, P. (1997), *The Actor Speaks*, London: Methuen Drama.

Shakespeare, William (1995), *The Sonnets and A Lovers Complaint*, London: Penguin Classics.
Shakespeare, William (2010), *The Complete Works of Shakespeare: The Arden Shakespeare*, London: Bloomsbury.
Turner, J. C. (2007), *Voice and Speech in the Theatre*, 6th edn, ed. Jane Boston, London: A&C Black.

5 Articulation Through Inspired Laban Efforts

> If the tongue had not been framed for articulation, man would still be a beast in the forest. *RALPH WALDO EMERSON*

Articulation meanings:

1. The formation of clear speech.
2. The articulation of consonants.
3. To enunciate.

Introduction

In this chapter, we will explore, deepen and clarify what is meant by dynamic articulation. We will discover how Laban Efforts support improvement of the quality of articulation and understand bodywork in relation to articulation of movement.

Rudolf Laban (1879–1958) was a dancer of Hungarian descent, a pioneer of modern dance, creating theoretical innovations in dance and choreography known as the Laban movement analysis. He founded the Laban Art movement in London, and the Trinity Laban *conservatoire* continues his legacy today. He used eight ways to articulate the body: wring, dab, float, glide, punch, flick, press and slash.

The sounds of speech are produced in the processes of breathing, phonation, oro-nasal resonance and articulation.

Some move, such as the vocal folds, the lips, tongue, velum (soft palate), the uvula, the pharynx and the jaw, and there are also the fixed articulators, the teeth, hard palate, the alveolar ridge. Inspiring the thought to initiate the breath to use the speech to deliver a line supports dynamic articulation.

To quote the French philosopher Jean de la Bruyère (1645–1696), 'There are certain things in which mediocrity is not to be endured, such as poetry, music, painting, and public speaking.'

Body, senses, tongue, ears

Feel the work: The body

Exercise 1: Warm up the body

Move around the space, using your body to explore curves; curves in space, curves in the body, the legs, the arms, the hands, and the head and neck. Explore this and release a breath for 1 minute.

Now move around the space, exploring how much movement is in the articulation of the joints, from the joints of your body, the knees, the ankles, the wrists, the elbows, the shoulders, the neck.

Explore this and release a breath for 1 minute.

Now imagine fire under your feet as you move around the space.

Explore and release a breath for 1 minute.

Exercise 2: The senses

Exploring the senses, stand in a neutral relaxed pose. Gently tap your face with your fingers to bring blood to the surface of the skin, making you aware of what faces the world. Practice this for 1 minute.

Next massage your face around the cheeks and jaw, this will make you aware of the muscles and tension in the face. Explore this for 1 minute.

Finally, place your fingers down the sides of your nose and sniff, this will make you aware of your nasal cavity.

Exercise 3: The lips and tongue

Exploring the lips, blow through the lips without sound (lip trills), try this for 1 minute.

Now blow through the lips with sound (horse lips), try this for 1 minute, bringing awareness to your lips.

Next move your tongue around the inside of your mouth.

Now move your tongue outside your mouth, allowing it to be stiff like a diving board.

Next allow the tongue to be floppy, like wet lettuce.

Now try speaking some well-rehearsed text with a floppy tongue and notice how this feels.

Finally, speak some text with a very rigid tongue like a diving board and notice how this feels.

Exercise 4: The jaw, ears, neck and scalp

Exploring the jaw release is often helpful to understand how jaw tension affects speech. You may often find with the shoulders, neck and back tension a feeling that you may also experience jaw tension. You may have clenched your teeth or have bruxism, which is grinding the teeth. You may have experienced jaw tension that creates headaches, tinnitus, upper back, shoulder and neck pain, especially after waking. Adopting a daily practice to release this tension will support the rest of your articulation.

Start by sitting or standing in a neutral pose.

Lay the hands over the ears and close your eyes and take a few deep breaths.

Take your v fingers, that is your forefinger and middle finger, then create an opening with your ring finger and little finger (think Dr Spock hand gesture from *Star Trek*, which is also an emoji) and place them either side of your ears and rub up and down. Take a deep breath in and out and notice how this feels to give attention to areas of tension and release.

Next take your fingers in a slight pinching motion and massage very gently all around your outer ear. These are sensitive areas that connect to the neuro pathways.

Continue to massage the ear and come to the lower lobe of your ear towards the top of your jawbone. Lightly massage in small circles. Do this for 1 minute each way, both clockwise and anticlockwise.

Now brush the jaw down slowly with the palms of your hands.

Next take your fingertips underneath the cheek muscles (this is the major chewing muscle, the masseter), gently push upwards and hold the fingertips there, noticing if you feel any discomfort, however slight, and it will allow some release of tension.

Now take your thumbs and place them under the chin to where your tongue sits inside and give it a little massage and breathe through this, allowing a sigh to escape.

Now gently massage the jaw area, and that includes the masseter muscles on the lower portion of the cheeks.

Next massage around the face towards the ears in an outward motion. This will release any lymphatic drainage towards the outer area of your face and jaw.

Brush down the sides of your jaw and release on a sigh.

Keep your lower jaw in a relaxed place with your mouth gently open. Expire a breath on a sigh of relief.

Exercise 5: Scalp

Next take your fingers up towards to your temples and massage little circles one way and then the other. This can release headaches, but notice what works for you.

Now with your fingertips or knuckles, massage around your temporalis, which is above and behind the ear. Imagine this area is like a seashell as you massage this area.

Now massage the scalp by taking the fingers and lift the face and hair as you massage your fingers through your hair. You are taking the fascia over the cranial bones, working from the outside towards the centre of your scalp. Massage the scalp and back of the head into the occiput (back of the head).

Next, if you can, grab your hair and give it a gentle pull in an upwards motion, then pull the hair out to the sides, and finally grab your hair and pull in a downwards motion.

Now massage the back and top and sides of the head and base of the skull with your thumbs, and release the jaw at the same time, expire a breath and escape on a sigh of relief.

Next walk around the room keeping the jaw open and let out a sigh of joy. Notice when the tension wants to creep back in.

Exercise 6: Soft palate

Soft palate the sun-brella rise and fall
I call this the sun-brella exercise. Sit or stand in neutral with your eyes closed. As you raise and lower the soft palette, imagine the sun shining at the back of your mouth onto your soft palette. Allow the soft palette to feel like an umbrella raising and lowering to allow the sun in or to give you shade.

Exercise 7: The tongue

Try rolling your tongue forwards and backwards, without sound. This is sometimes known as slug tongue or the wave. Keeping your jaw passive and open, try to keep your jaw fairly still without being rigid, and roll the tongue in a wave in and out with the tip of the tongue touching the bottom teeth. Allow the body of the tongue to move outwards.

Next try the same tongue roll, wave or slug with sound. Again, keep the jaw fairly still, only this time allow a sound to escape. I suggest 'Yeah Yeah Yeah'.

Next try circling the tongue ten times on one side of the cheek, then the other way, before repeating on the other side. Notice if your neck wants to thrust forward.

If you can, try twisting your tongue from side to side. You may wish to use a mirror to see how much your head and neck want to engage.

Tips for teachers

Jaw relaxation in class can focus the mind on body parts. It also creates time to focus on how the students feel. Often, they might frown or show in their faces some element of discomfort, which you can then support further. It is useful in these exercises to constantly remind your students to keep the jaw relaxed.

Warm-up articulators

Exercise 8: Physical articulation

Move around your space, imagining and physicalising the game of playing basketball as you bounce a ball, and make the /b/ buh sound as you bounce the ball around. Try this for 1 minute.

Now physicalise playing imaginary badminton as you produce the puh sound. Try this for 1 minute.

Next explore the /t/ tuh sound, physicalising that you are typing on a keyboard. Do this for 1 minute.

Next explore the /d/ duh sound, physicalising that you are dabbing paint on a wall. Try this for 1 minute.

Now say the /k/ kuh sound, physicalising that you are stroking a cat. Try this for 1 minute.

Now explore the sound /g/ guh, physicalising that you are swallowing a large drink. Try this for 1 minute.

Try out all the following consonants whilst physicalising the following movements.

> Physicalise playing bow and arrows and making the /f/ sound.
>
> Next physicalise playing with a machine that makes toys and make the /v/ sound.
>
> Now physicalise being a snake and make the /s/ sound.
>
> Next physicalise a bee sting and make the /z/ sound.
>
> Finally, physical being under the shower and make the /sh/ sound.

Tips for teachers

These warm-ups create an understanding of the energy placed on consonants. This is an effective way to warm up the articulators and engages the students. It also allows some playfulness and movement qualities. Your students could use this as homework and produce their own versions of what each sound is and share this with the class.

Consonants

Feel the work: Bilabial plosives /p/ and /b/

Exercise 9

Now say puh as in the /p/ sound. You should feel an explosion of air as it escapes the lips. Try it several times on the back of your hand to feel the air pressure. Notice this is a voiceless sound.

Now say buh as in the /b/ sound. You will notice this is a voiced sound and you may even feel vibrations in your throat area. Place one hand on your throat and explore the /buh sound.

Practice the work: /p/ and /b/

Words with /p/ in the front of the word (initial position):
Positive perms for parents make proud people.

Words with /p/ in the middle of the word (medial position):
Happy hopping hips.

Words with /p/ at the end of a word (final position):
Stop shop pop.

Words with /b/ in the initial position:
Bunting bought bounced beautifully.
Rubbing tubby cabby.

Words with /b/ in the final position:
Blurb crab kebab stab.

Practice the work further: /p/ and /b/ (sentences)

Both potential balloons and beach balls are potent in both pong and ping as pairs. Back when balancing blue balloons, they became bouncy, but pink beach balls will babble and baffle the big bouncy balloon with a boing. Pixy the pilot bounced the plane in the plaza on a plume of blue and pink pandas.

Understand the work: /p/ and /b/

/p/ and /b/ are voiced and voiceless bilabial plosives. This means that when the lips come together, they form an obstruction to the outflowing breath, then pressure builds up behind the lips and when suddenly open or free, sound is produced. If the vocal folds are vibrating the sound will be voiced as in the sound /b/; or if they are not vibrating, the sound will be voiceless as in the sound /p/.

Feel the work: Alveolar plosives
Exercise 10

Say tuh as in the /t/ sound.

Practice the work: /t/ voiceless

Words in the initial position:
   Tuneful tyrants take turkey to task.

Words in the medial position:
   Netted knitting was nasty for the country.

Words in the final position:
   Eat the plate cat or do not fight cat eight.

Now say duh as in the /d/ sound.

Practice the work: /d/ voiced

Words in initial position:
   Do not do dirty dishes.

Words in medial position:
   Under ladders adorn adders.

Words in final position:
   Wood wind wound bird.

Practice the work further: /t/ and /d/ (sentences)

Terry should turn down the treat offered to him by Tony the tetchy Tiger during Tuesday's ladder cat test. Tadpoles are testy on Tuesday, but Terry chose to take the treat from Tony. This turned Terry into a terrible tizz. Because on Tuesday tadpoles cannot have treats as it is a time for taking the turtle Tiffany to town. Terry was late and Tiffany was very cross at the turn of events.

Understand the work: /t/ and /d/

/t/ and /d/ alveolar plosives sounds are made when the tip of the tongue contacts the alveolar ridge and pulls back quickly, this sudden movement of tongue creates a release of airflow creating the /t/ and /d/ sound. One is voiced and one is voiceless.

Feel the work: The velar plosives /k/ and /g/

Exercise 11

Now say guh as in the /g/ sound.

Next say kuh as in the /k/ sound.

Feel the work: The voiceless /k/

Words in the initial position.
   Keep kitten in kegs for comfort in the kitchen.

Words in the medial position.
   Parking the parkers with crackers, using napkins.

Words in the final position:
   Break the black bike and blink.

Feel the work: The voiced /g/

Words in the initial position:
   Go get the girls gifts.

Words in the medial position:
   Aggro from Aggie was fugal.

Words in the final position:
   Big bug was a cog in a fog.

Practice the work further: /k/ and /g/ (sentences)

Khaki curtains and cushions were caught on camera with a kangaroo grunting to gain good connections and comedy for the gold conkers, which gazed at the glazy kangaroos.

Understand the work: /k/ and /g/

On the out breath as the soft palate rises it closes off the nasal pathway. As the back of the tongue touches the soft palate, it stops the air from escaping. As there is a build up of air pressure the tongue then relaxes, and the pressure is released.

Feel the work: /f/ and /v/ fricatives
Exercise 12

Now say vuh as in the /v/ sound.
Next say fuh as in the /f/ sound.

Feel the work: Voiceless /f/

Words in the initial position:
   Finally found funny fabulous Fred.

Words in the medial position:
   Muffy fluffy trifle after softly fifty jiffy.

Words in the final position:
   Chief Cliff, bluff aloof.

Feel the work: Voiced /v/

Words in the initial position:
   Vests value vision vanity.

Words in the medial position:
   Havoc over duvets given gavel.

Words in the final position:
   Improve shove satnav drive drove.

Practice the work further: /f/ and /v/ (sentences)

Valid vampires voted for foxes, as they were valued because of their faded valour to fake fires and save a favour. Very funny fable which is factually fact.

Understand the work: /f/ and /v/

The top teeth come into contact with the lower lip. There is a build-up of air pressure which forces the air to rush through, making a friction sound.

Feel the work: Voiceless dental fricatives /th/

Words in the initial position:
   Theatre was a thing to think of thirty thousand thoughts.

Words in the medial position:
   Author's toothache is a birthday.

Words in the final position:
   Earth and tooth are month math.

Feel the work: Voiced dental fricatives /th/
Exercise 14

Words in the initial position:
   Then their thou.

Words in the medial position:
   Mothers brother was a southerner.

Words in the final position:
   Soothe the smooth.

Practice the work further: /th/ voiced and voiceless (sentences)

Those teeth that were unearthed thought that the thistles mother was this thoughtful thankful, method actor. This caused those to question thee, thou and thy.

Understand the work

The blade of the tongue touches the top teeth forcing air through due to the obstruction, on the exhalation making a friction-like sound.

Feel the work: Alveolar fricatives /s/ and /z/

Now say zuh as in the /z/ sound.
Finally, say suh as in the /s/ sound.

Feel the work: Voiceless /s/

Words in the initial position:
   Silly sue saw the sore on Sophie and soothed it.

Words in the medial position:
Lucy lanced the dusty disc in the basin.

Words in the final position:
Pious mess at once is basis.

Feel the work: Voiced /z/

Words in the initial position:
Zillions of zones zoom the zigzag.

Words in the medial position:
Bazar kazoos are a zzz.

Words in the final position:
Has jazz hertz or quartz.

Practice the work: /s/ and /z/ further (sentences)

Suzy saw the zany zesty side of zippy and Sophie on Saturday, but also said Zoe saw the snorkel in snowy Zanzibar. Zone out Sophie said, but Zoe chose to silence Sophie and Suzy with a silly song.

Understand the work

An obstruction caused by the blade of the tongue touches the alveolar ridge, this then builds air pressure to force air to rush and create a friction sound.

Exercise 16: Nasals m, n and ng

Feel the work: /m/ the bilabial nasal

Two lips come together to form the closure and sound escapes through the nose creating resonance.

Words in the initial position:
   Masters of minds make money.

Words in the medial position:
   Amounts amend the camping.

Words in the final position:
   Harm and farm are a charm.

Feel the work: /n/ the alveolar nasal
Exercise 17

These are created when the blade of the tongue touches the alveolar ridge. The tongue stays in this location and air is released through the nose.

Words in the initial position:
   Nosey knights are naughty.

Words in the medial position:
   Pennies and pinecones are a picnic.

Words in the final position:
   Phone the crone and be alone.

Practice the work further: /m/ and /n/ (sentences)

Meisner like many other moles gathered on Mondays at noon. Moles like Meisner repeated many names, to gather information about other moles in the vicinity. Waiting for other moles to arrive, Meisner spotted an otter, 'Don't come round here' said Meisner to the otter who was on the bank of the river Rhud. 'It's dangerous for you to be here especially on a Monday.' The otter paused and looked longingly at the river, 'But I like to be by the river,' she said, 'it is warm, windy, and wet, and besides, I do not know what a Monday is.' Meisner the mole walked up and down and huffed a bit before replying, 'If you come on Tuesday – that is tomorrow or any other day then that will be fine, just not on a Monday. A Monday is the day that is called after the weekend.' Otter replied, 'But I don't know what the days are called, and I don't know when I should not come.' 'Oh dear, oh dear', said Meisner the mole, 'didn't you go to otter school?' 'No', said the otter, 'we stayed at home and built dams.'

Understand the work

Nasal resonance occurs when there is an obstruction as the soft palate lowers and there is closure of the oral cavity, so the air flows out through the nose.

Feel the work: The velar nasal /ng/

Exercise 17

Words in the medial position:
   Anger and linger the finger and hunger.

Words in the final position:
   The song is sung with a ping and a pong.

Practice the work further: /ng/ (sentences)

The Singer's tongue, bringing along a song, was sounding young, and her single was a tingle, flinging the wrong song she was stung, by a ponging pinging ringing.

Understand the work

The oral cavity is blocked by the back of the tongue against the soft palate and air flows through the nose. The voiced velar nasal is a nasal consonant.

Practice the work further

W as in initial position: Wendy went to work on Wednesday.
W as in medial position: twenty twirly swans.
I in initial position: lucky lucy learnt of London.
I in medial position: always alone below.
I in final position: tall fall mall.
R in initial position: ready run and ran.
R in medial position: around agree arrows.
Sh: sheds and showers shuffle.
Ch: cheep chips in Chelsea.
Dj: Jordan joked about Julie.
Y: yeah, yesterday you used yoke.

Laban efforts of movement, breath, sound and text

Rudolph Laban used his method and language to describe and interpret human movement. He taught that there are four basic elements of movement which he called Motion Factors of space, weight, time and flow, and these create the following followed by the eight combinations which are known as: float, punch (or thrust), glide, dab, flick, wring and press. His aim was to help actors and dancers to express movement through experimentation, allowing the actor to focus on the effort not the thought.

Warm up for Laban Efforts (video)

I like to work with Laban Efforts in a manner of body, breath, sound and speech. Therefore, each of these instructions can be done singularly or you can combine them. However, I feel that truly exploring how the body reacts to a physical impulse fully allows you to explore the full range of motions that can affect the sounds. I begin with a physical warm up using the movements of direct or indirect, the weight of heavy or light, the speed of quick, slow or sustained and flow of bound or free.

Exercise 19: Warm up

First move around the space in a direct way (you know where you are going), notice your breath and release a sound that describes how you feel. Try this for 1 minute.

Now move around the space in an indirect way (you may not know where you are going), notice your breath and release a sound or a word that describes how you feel. Try this for 1 minute.

Next move around the space and imagine the weight of heaviness in your body. Release a sound or a word that describes how you feel. Try this for 1 minute.

Now move around the space and imagine the weight of lightness in your body. Release a sound or a word that describes how you feel. Try this for 1 minute.

Next move around the space and explore with a fast speed in your body. Release a sound or a word that describes how you feel. Try this for 1 minute.

Next walk around the space and explore a slow movement in your body. Release a sound or a word. Try this for 1 minute.

Now walk around the space and explore the sustained movement in your body, such as pushing something across the space. Release a sound or a word that describes how you feel. Try this for 1 minute.

Next walk around the space and notice a bound movement in your body, such as being held back. Release a sound or a word that describes how you feel. Try this for 1 minute.

Finally, walk around the space and notice a flowing movement in your body. Release a sound or a word that describes how you feel. Try this for 1 minute.

Now that we have looked at the motion factors, we will now explore the Laban Efforts in breath, sound and speech.

Exercise 20: Laban, tongue and text

Using a mirror begin to explore your tongue and the sounds listed.

Dab the tip of your tongue in and out, next dab the sound /dah/ as in dab.

Slash your tongue in and out, slashing out the sound /slah/ as in slash.

Flick your tongue in and out, flicking out the sound /flih/ as in flick.

Float your tongue in and out, floating out the sound /floh/ as in float.

Press your tongue in and out, pressing out the sound /preh/ as in press.

Wring your tongue in and out, wringing out the sound /rih/ as in wring.

Punch or thrust your tongue in and out, punch out the sound /pu/ as in punch.

Glide your tongue in and out, gliding out the sound /glih/gli/gli as in glide.

You may notice all the sounds are the beginnings of each of the Laban Efforts.

Understand the work

The tongue is a fabulous big fat muscle. It is made up of four paired intrinsic and four paired extrinsic muscles. The intrinsic muscles can change the shape and size of the tongue from diving board to floppy lettuce shape we did earlier, and the muscle helps with swallowing, eating and speaking. The extrinsic muscles create shape, with the ability to stick the tongue in and out and pull it down and up, supporting up and down motion and side to side.

Feel the work: Movement, breath, sound, text (video)

With each effort listed, move around the space, using your hand or arm or motion of the head or leg. Allow yourself to experience each of the following efforts, the sequence is as follows: movement, breath, sound then text.

Exercise 21

Float your body around the space, and expire the breath, followed by a sound, then express the words, 'I float'.

Dab your body around the room and expire the breath, followed by a sound, then express the words, 'I dab'.

Wring your body, arms and legs, expire the breath, followed by a sound, then express the words 'I wring'.

Punch or thrust your body around the room, expire the breath, followed by a sound, then express the words, 'I punch' or ' I thrust'.

Press the body, using your arms and legs, in all directions, expire the breath, followed by a sound, then express the words 'I press'.

Flick the body in all directions, expiring the breath, followed by a sound, then express the words, 'I flick'.

Slash the body in all directions, expiring the breath, followed by a sound, then express the words, 'I slash'.

Glide the body around the room, expiring breath, followed by a sound, then express the words, 'I glide'.

Notice how each effort has its own unique physical and vocal characteristic.

Do you like being in some efforts more than others? If so, why? Does the rhythm or physical effort correspond to something you are more familiar with?

Now try using the Laban Efforts both physically and vocally with some text with which you are familiar. Or try the sonnet listed. I have added Laban Efforts.

Sonnet 85

My tongue-tied Muse in manners holds her still, (wring or press)
While comments of your praise, richly compiled, (float)
Reserve their character with golden quill, (flick)
And precious phrase by all the Muses filed. (slash)
I think good thoughts, whilst other write good words, (dab)
And, like unlettered clerk, still cry 'Amen' (dab)
To every hymn that able spirit affords (float)
In polished form of well- refined pen. (glide)
Hearing you praised, I say 'tis so, tis true,' (flick)
And to the most of praise add something more; (float)
But that is in my thought whose love to you, (glide)
Though words come hindmost holds his rank before. (slash)
Then others for the breath of words respect, (flick)
Me for my dumb thoughts, speaking in effect. (press)

What do the Laban Efforts do to the text? Does it change the intention? Clarify the intention? How does it affect the voice in terms of pitch, tune, range, articulation or breath?

Understand the work

Combining Laban Efforts with articulation creates a more dynamic and expressive speech. For example, the Laban Effort Punch, where some of the movements might suggest forceful articulation and emphatic speech. Float movements can support gentle or soothing elements of speech, especially in sustained sounds. Glide might suggest a steady, calm, fluid rhythm of speech, whilst the Slash Effort, like the Punch, could enhance passion, shifts of tone or volume. By working through the Efforts, it is possible to have a greater variety of choices to explore as an actor, as you continue to develop your craft. It can support and underpin gestures with intensity which in turn amplifies the vocal variety of speech, developing internal thoughts and reflecting outward feelings embodied in voice and movement.

Practice the work

Try your own Laban Efforts on the sonnet.

Next, I have set out a Laban Effort for each line of the Shakespeare monologue from *Richard III*. I have offered suggestions of each line with a different Laban Effort; these may work for you.

Repeat the exercise changing the Efforts I have suggested until you settle on the right one for you. Notice how it affects the language, the pace, the weight, the direction. Also notice the choices it gives you, the actor, the ability to play a varied approach to what you offer.

Richard III:

Was ever woman in this humour woo'd? FLOAT
Was ever woman in this humour won? GLIDE
I'll have her, but I will not keep her long. PRESS
What? I, that kill'd her husband and his father, THRUST/
   PUNCH

To take her in her heart's extremest hate, SLASH
With curses in her mouth, tears in her eyes, FLICK
The bleeding witness of my hatred by; WRING
Having God, her conscience, and these bars against me,
    FLICK
And I no friends to back my suit at all, PRESS
But the plain devil and dissembling looks, DAB
And yet to win her! All the world to nothing! PUNCH
Ha! FLICK
Hath she forgot already that brave prince, PUNCH/THRUST
Edward, her lord, whom I, some three months since,
    FLICK
Stabbed in my angry mood at Tewksbury? SLASH
A sweeter and a lovelier gentleman, GLIDE
Fram'd in the prodigality of nature, GLIDE
Young, valiant, wise, and (no doubt) right royal, FLICK
The spacious world cannot again afford. FLOAT
And will she yet abase her eyes on me, WRING
That cropp'd the golden prime of this sweet prince PUNCH
And made her widow to a woeful bed? GLIDE
On me, whose all not equals Edward's moiety? FLOAT
On me, that halts and am misshapen thus? SLASH
My dukedom to a beggarly denier, DAB
I do mistake my person all this while! SLASH
Upon my life, she finds (although I cannot) DAB
Myself to be a marvellous proper man. GLIDE
I'll be at charges for a looking-glass, GLIDE
And entertain a score or two of tailors PRESS
To study fashions to adorn my body: FLOAT
Since I am crept in favour with myself, FLICK
I will maintain it with some little cost. FLICK
But first I'll turn yon fellow in his grave; PUNCH/THRUST
And then return lamenting to my love. GLIDE
Shine out, fair sun, till I have bought a glass, FLOAT
That I may see my shadow as I pass. PRESS

Now try a monologue of your own choosing, applying the Laban Efforts, first with breath, then sound, followed by the speaking of the text. Notice any changes in your articulation and in how you deliver the text. You may wish to try a short scene with someone where you are clear about each Laban Effort for each line. Notice how it affects the scene, the articulation and pace of the speech, potentially the pitch.

Suggested texts

Benjamin Zephaniah, 'Everybody is doing it' (1980), *Pen Rythm Collection*, London: Bloodaxe.

Michael Niflis, *Movement* (1973), Chicago: Poetry Foundation.

Further reading

Baker, H. (2014), *The Sunshine Kid*, Bristol: Burning Eye Books.

Bloom, K. and Shreeves, R. (1998), *Moves*, London: Routledge.

Carey, D. and Clark Carey, R. (2010), *The Verbal Arts Workbook*, London: Methuen Drama UK.

Jung, C. translated by Hull, R. F. C. (1991), *The Archetypes and the Collective Unconscious*, London: Taylor and Francis Ltd.

Morrison, Annie (2022), *A Moment in Speech*, London: Methuen Drama.

Newlove, J. (1993), *Laban for Actors and Dancers*, London: Nick Hern Books.

Rodgers, J., ed. (2002), *The Complete Voice and Speech Workout*, Montclair, NJ: Applause.

Tempest, Kae (2016), *Let Them Eat Chaos*, Picador, UK.

Tempest, Kae (2021), *Paradise*, Picador, UK.

Shakespeare, William (1995), *The Sonnets and A Lovers Complaint*, London: Penguin Classics UK.

Shakespeare, William (2010), *The Complete Works of Shakespeare: The Arden Shakespeare*, London: Bloomsbury.

6 Resonance – Meisner Inspired

> I think people who vibrate at the same frequency, vibrate towards each other. They call it, in science, sympathetic vibrations. ERYKAH BADU

Resonance definitions:

1 Deep quality of sound reverberating.
2 Pronunciation of a sound as a result of vibrations.
3 Resonance is presence.
4 A quality evoking a response.

Introduction

In this chapter we will examine the resonance in voice work, creating presence to deliver power, whilst deepening the connection to the authentic self, through the Meisner Acting Technique. Resonance can mean a lot of different things to people: a vibration caused by sound waves, the vibrating sound of a voice, through phonemic contribution to the timbre of the voice, resonance with another human being through a shared connection. An amplifier for sound, it carries the sound waves.

What is the Meisner technique and how can it affect the voice?

Sanford Meisner was an actor trainer, teaching alongside Lee Strasberg in New York. Meisner's actor training method was originally developed from the practice of Konstantin Stanislavski. However, unlike the former actor trainer who originally used the actors' own emotions to create a truthful experience on stage,

Meisner chose to formulate a principle based on the interaction with the other person on stage and find a connection and impulse through the other actor.

What defined acting for Sanford Meisner was to 'live as truthfully', under 'imaginary circumstances'. He felt that the fundamental areas affecting young actors is that they feel exposed and self-conscious. To him, that meant that they were only pretending to pay attention to the scenes or the other person whilst actually planning their next line. Therefore, not responding to the given circumstance.

Of course, his style of training changed, evolved, and moved into a process that one thinks of his method based on repetition alone.

Warm-up resonance

Feel the work: Warm-up resonance
Exercise 1: The five-sided box exercise

Lie on the floor on your (left) side with your knees bent and explore humming using a range of notes whilst always keeping your jaw open and relaxed but your lips pursed closed. Stay her for 3 minutes then open your mouth to an AH sound as in car.

Now lie on your back and repeat the hum, exploring other notes for 3 minutes, then open your mouth to an AH.

Next lie on your other side (right) and repeat the hum for 3 minutes then open your mouth to an AH sound.

Now lie on your belly and continue to hum for 3 minutes exploring a few notes and then open your mouth to the AH sound.

Next come up to sitting and explore the hum for 3 minutes and open the mouth to the AH sound.

Now speak some text and notice the resonance you may feel vibrating in your chest. Your speaking note may be lower or higher than you usually speak.

Understand the work

When the vocal tract shapes sound to match natural frequencies, it amplifies tones. From the power of the hum with a closed mouth it is possible to feel the resonance as it vibrates through the body. When opening the mouth to a vowel sound, we begin to hear the sound through resonance, allowing for greater vocal projection.

Practice the work

Here are some exercises you can do alone. With many of these exercises it is useful to record yourself prior to the work to get an idea of how your voice feels before starting the voice work, and where it sits after. This gives you a benchmark to work from. You can make a mental note of the quality of the sound and the vibrations you feel, through the vowels. Notice the difference in the long and short vowels.

Exercise 2

Note the long vowels listed and how they sound, exploring the length of the vowel. Explore the sounds placing one hand on the chest and feel the vibration. Intone each vowel sound.

OO as in tune.

OH as bow.

AW as in law.

AH as in car.

AYE as in pay.

EE as in me.

Repeat the exercise, changing notes, and placing one hand on the back of your neck feel any vibrations.

Next place your hand on your nasal area and see if you can feel any vibrations.

Would you rate the sound as warm? Colourful? Exciting? Powerful?

You might wish to rate yourself before the exercises listed, and after the vocal work.

Exercise 3: Oyster shell (video)

Lie on the floor on your right side with your knees bent, palm to palm, gently humming. As the hum begins to grow stronger allow the sound to open to a vowel such as an AH. As the sound is released take the top arm and top leg over to the other side allowing you to close the lips and express the hum again.

Now repeat the exercise on the other side, humming until the sound grows in volume in order to allow you to express an open vowel. Allow the top arm and bent knee to propel you to the left side.

This is a wonderful exercise that supports a sustained sound and an experience of constant slow motion and sound.

Figure 6.1 Suppress the alien.

Exercise 4: Suppress the alien

This next exercise is similar in movement to the oyster shell, only the movements to propel you from one side to the other are much faster.

Hum to AH to hum.

Lie curled on your right side with your knees bent, gently humming, and hold your belly. Imagine that an alien is inside your belly area, and its sound is throbbing through you like a hum. You are looking after this alien much like the boy Elliot in the film *E.T.* by Stephen Spielberg. The humming alien inside you (the alien) gets stronger and stronger until you can no longer suppress it, and it forces you to lie flat on your back releasing an 'ah' sound, sending the sound up to the sky, as a call to its ship. After some time, you can force the sound back to a hum by curling onto the opposite side, the left side.

Next, lying on the left side repeat the exercise of hum to an AH then back to a hum.

Understand the work

By feeling and hearing how strong a vocal hum can feel through vibrations, you are able to realise and appreciate how much energy, and vocal power, the hum can have, before you are forced to let out a sound by opening the mouth and sending the sound up to the sky, or the ceiling, or universe, calling out to the spaceship.

Sit up and speak some text.

Notice the volume and power in your voice.

Practice the work

Try the exercise a few times.

Now imagine the alien forces you to stand on your feet allowing you to explore sound to the world. Feel the power of the fully opened body and sound and you can no longer suppress the alien.

Understand it

How often have we listened to the voices that advertise an action film? What about the villains of many films or the romantic leads that often carry wonderful resonance that make us shudder or quiver in equal measures, perhaps unconsciously registering their resonance and feeling the quality of the actor's voice practically coming through the TV, radio or YouTube channel as if it is trembling! Some famous voices easily recognisable for example are Morgan Freeman's, his voice is an example of fully rounded and delightful resonance, as is Brian Cox, Patrick Stewart, James Earl Jones, and the equally female resonant voices of Judi Dench, Cate Blanchett, Viola Davis. A voiceover on an advert creates a mood of warmth or power that can stimulate and excite you. In my previous book I mention that I imagine the voice quality being 3-D as an image in sound, that without resonance the voice can feel quite flat and thin. I like to think of the voice radiating colours with waves of heat and light coming from all parts of your body, that radiation of energy sending vibrations out to the other person you are working with.

How do we create vibrations in our voice to evoke a response? Can this be the source of volume and power?

Exercise 5: The glass pyramid

Imagine you have been beamed up to a spaceship by your friend the alien. They have put you in a glass pyramid.

Stand in a wide-legged stance, where you feel that your body is well balanced. The nice alien is inviting you to create three sounds that they wish you to explore in order to communicate with them. You are volunteering to help the communication

Figure 6.2 Stuck in a glass pyramid.

between you, our world, and this new species. They want you to create enough sound to shatter the glass through resonance.

First, the alien suggests the sound you make at your lowest note is the OH sound, much like the sound a bear might make, around the lower part of your body. Explore the OH sound deep in your range and extend and elongate that vowel sound.

The alien suggests you use your arms to explore this sound further to break the glass. The alien wants to time you to make the sound for 2 minutes.

Next, the alien suggests the sound you make is the AH sound, working in the middle of your range and the middle of your body available to you today, as you try to shatter the glass.

Once again, the alien suggests 2 minutes in this sound and use your arms across your chest and out to the sides of the pyramid.

Finally, the alien wants you to explore the EE sound which works in the upper register of your voice, as you try to shatter the glass and use your arms to try and reach the top of the pyramid.

The alien is suggesting 2 minutes in this sound, and finally imagine that you have shattered the glass pyramid.

Listening and feeling the exercise with instant feedback.

Voice funnels

Exercise 6: Voice funnel

Figure 6.3 Voice funnel.

You can buy at any supermarket a cylindrical tube filled with crisp snacks. You may wish to personalise this as you see in the photo. Once you have your funnel, gently hold it at the bottom with the fingers of one hand and with the other hand hold the body of the funnel, again hold very lightly.

Hold it about an inch from your mouth and explore an open vowel such as an 'ah' sound. Instantly you should feel how the voice funnel vibrates on one or two notes. Explore the sound further with different notes and see where you feel the work vibrate and where you cannot.

Now explore the lips trills with a continuous drone like sound.

Next create upper and lower pitch variations, always feeling if the voice funnel vibrates.

Now explore sound with an open continuous vowel sound, such as an AH, and see if your partner can hear or feel the vibrations.

Now continuing to hold the voice funnel, imagine the sound vibrating through your chest. You may need to play around with different notes to feel the voice funnel vibrate.

You may wish to place one hand on your chest to feel any vibrations which may give you some physical feedback.

Next explore the sustained AH sound or the sustained OH sound placing one hand on your head. Notice any vibratory feedback.

Now try exploring the sustained OH sound or the sustained AH sound using a variety of notes around the back of the neck, and feel any shivers, shakes or vibrations.

Finally, place two fingers gently on one side of your nose and see if the voice funnel or your fingers vibrate, then repeat on the other side of your nose.

You may need to play with pitch or vowel sounds in order to place the sound in these different areas, but you will begin to feel the vibrations and explore fully the resonance.

Practice voice funnel in pairs.

Exercise 7: In pairs, funnels

In pairs, begin to explore the sounds of sustained OH and AH again, only this time your partner will feel the vibrations on the bottom and sides of their voice funnel.

They are receiving the sound and listening to the sound that you are offering.

They then respond to sound you have given by repeating your sound back to you.

Keep this exercise going where Partner (A) makes sound and Partner (B) Repeats this sound back to (A). Allow for listening and changes in pitch or pace. Do not force the change, this is really about truly listening to what is being offered, before responding.

Understand the work

The voice funnel acts as a conductor of sound waves, called acoustic propagation. When sound is produced through the voice funnel it creates vibrations in the air molecules and when the voice funnel vibrates it causes movement in the particles of air, called sound waves. When you hold the funnel gently you will feel through your fingers the bounce of the sound waves. The sound vibrates much like the barrel of your chest and allows the potential for a greater degree of volume and power. This conductor also acts to resonate the sound out to the audience. When you are resonating fully it is almost impossible to sound breathy. This exercise was first introduced to me by the vocal coach David Carey.

Tips for teachers

I have taken this exercise with the tubes one step further, by calling it a voice funnel and where students create their own unique cover. It allows them the opportunity to invest in the idea of the voice funnel. Many of my students recognise the volume, power, amplification and rapid oscillations they get by using this to support the principles of resonance. You can organise your group into a circle, then allow them all to create open vowel sounds into the funnel, whilst one person stands in the middle with their eyes closed and begins to feel the sound through the funnel as well as through their ears. They can feel the vibrations of others. This receiving and responding helps deepen the principles of listening and responding through repetition. This can also be a wonderful sound bath.

Repetition in resonance

Feel the work: Meisner, resonance and presence

Exercise 8: Robotic repetition, the self

I have used southern British vowels for this exercise.

First relax the mouth and jaw.

Repeat each of the following sounds for 1 minute to feel the structural energy of the lips, jaw and mouth opening.

Explore the OO sound and repeat for 1 minute. Then create a list of words that have this sound and repeat over and over for one minute. Here are a few examples; OO as in ooze, booze, cruise, shoes, blues, news, fuse, loose, lose, spoon, choose, mousse, true.

Next explore the OH sound and repeat for 1 minute. Then create a list of words that have this sound and repeat over and over for 1 minute. Here are a few examples: no, show, glow, throw, foe, flow, toe, low, go.

Now explore the AW sound and repeat for 1 minute. Then create a list of words that have this sound and repeat over and over for 1 minute. Here are a few examples: shore, for, nor, gore, tor, law, sure, saw, thaw, crawl, tall, mall.

Next explore the OW sound and repeat for 1 minute. Then create a list of words that have this sound and repeat over and over for 1 minute. Here are a few examples: now, clown, brown, cow, frown, town.

Now explore the AH sound and repeat for 1 minute. Then create a list of words that have this sound and repeat over and over for 1 minute. Here are a few examples for you to try: car, farm, far, alarm, charm, task, grasp.

Understand it

The aim is to truly listen to the sounds you are making for a full minute. *Are you changing any of the sounds into words? Are you slightly shifting any of the mouth energy of the structure of the vowels?*

Try to keep the structure and integrity of the vowel.

You can feel the shape of the structure of each vowel from the smallest opening of the mouth in the vowel sound OO, to the largest opening in the vowel sound AH.

These exercises fully support a forward placed sound and aid a deeper, richer resonant quality of tone to the vowel sounds.

Listening and responding

Exercise 9: Robotic repetition, in pairs

In pairs, make a long vowel sound that can go back and forth between each other. Notice if the vowels change from their original concept of voicing.

To make this easier I have supplied some sounds in advance for you to repeat.

Partner (A) says Ah.

Partner (B) repeats exactly the Ah sound and the note as was expressed by Partner (A).

Partner (A) repeats back the Ah sound again.

Partner (B) repeats the Ah and so on – this can go on for a minute or so.

This exercise goes back and forth, listening and repeating what you heard exactly, not what you think you hear.

What can often happen in the first place is the need for Partner(A) to deliver the AH sound and <u>improve</u> the sound, rather than how it was given, and exactly as it was first sounded. However, if we are truly listening and responding then the sound would not change, but be exactly how it was given. So, the key is to repeat what you hear in this robotic listening, it reminds us of when we are not listening.

Practice the work: Listening, in pairs

Using the Shakespeare sonnet listed, explore listening to each other and find nuance in the words.

Sonnet 73

That times of year though mayst in me behold
When yellow leaves, or none, or few, do hang
Upon those boughs which shake against the cold,
Bare ruin'd choirs, where late the sweet birds sang.
In me thou see'st the twilight of such day
As after sunset fadeth in the west,
Which by and by black night doth take away,
Death's second self, that seals up all in rest.
In me though see'st the glowing of such fire
That on the ashes of his youth doth lie,
As the death-bed whereon it must expire,
Consum'd with that which it was nourish'd by.
This thou perceiv'st, which makes thy love more strong,
To love that well which thou must leave ere long.

Exercise 10: From robotic repetition to easy repetition

In pairs, Partner (A) makes a true comment that is personal to the opposite partner, such as: 'You are wearing red shoes', or 'Your tee-shirt is black', or 'Your glasses are blue'.

Partner (B) will say the personalised form of 'I am wearing red shoes', or 'My tee-shirt is black', therefore the comment is truthful for both parties, and here is where it gets interesting. Do not allow the intonation, pace or pitch to change. Respond to what they say and how they say it, listen for any variation.

Understand the work

This is first-level understanding of listen and repeat, which we did earlier with the voice funnels. It is a robotic repetition and does not really resemble any true listening or understanding, only enough to respond to, but important nevertheless to explore how we can become non-responsive if we do not truly listen. Meisner's repetition exercises may seem simple on the surface, involving actors to respond to each other's statements. However, the power lies in the continuous repetition, pushing performers to delve deeper into their emotional wellbeing and connect authentically with their scene partners. The exercises foster a profound understanding of the emotional life of a character and enhances an actor's ability to be present in the moment. This exploration of sounds enriches vocal expression, as does Meisner's repetitive exercises, deepening the emotional authenticity of actors. In order to repeat words or lines of a scene partner over and over again, the actor then listens and observes. The voice training and resonance through the Meisner Technique implies listening, observing and responding by focusing on someone other than the self, to evoke a response, which can only happen if one is truly listening and to be in the moment and present.

Exercise 11: Responding with active listening

Now the exercise is responding from your own point of view, allowing for variation and nuance.

Partner (A): 'You are wearing a green shirt' (for example).

Partner (B): 'I am wearing a green shirt.'

Next, explore this simple sentence of communication back and forth with your partner and notice how the response affects the sentence as you listen and respond.

Does it affect the emotional quality of the scene?

Learn to be tethered to the other person, this should feel like a dance, by receiving the impulse from the other person. The <u>effect</u> should <u>affect</u> the other person. Do not try and change or manipulate your partner, just listen, and focus on the scene partner. Change starts to happen in behaviours, allowing the scene partner to affect you, and is called 'being in the moment', not showing a rehearsal of what you have previously done.

Explore the scene below from *Much Ado About Nothing*, Act 1 Scene 1.

Exercise 12: Listening and responding with text

Try to actively listen before responding.

Benedick and Beatrice

Benedick: What, my dear Lady Disdain! Are you living?

Beatrice: Is it possible disdain should die, while she hath such meet food to feed it as Signior Benedick? Courtesy itself must convert to disdain, if you come in her presence.

Benedick: Then is courtesy a turncoat. But it is certain I am loved of all ladies, only you excepted: and I would, I could find in my heart that I had not a hard heart; for, truly, I love none.

Beatrice: A dear happiness to women; they would else have been troubled with a pernicious suitor. I thank God and my cold blood; I am of your humour for that: I had rather hear my dog bark at a crow than a man swear he loves me.

What do you notice about the listening aspect of this short scene? What does it tell you about the two characters?

Exercise 13: The imaginary orchestra (the self)

Pick up a metaphorical instrument listed below and play it using the sounds suggested. Vocalise each one for 2 minutes to truly feel the vibrations and resonance in each sound. Between each 'instrument' speak some text that you know, and acknowledge how each sound changes the resonance and pitch.

You may decide that each instrument is for a particular genre, if so, commit to this fully.

> Ukulele: with a fast tongue using the L sound as in la la la la la.
>
> Tambourine: explore the sound as in SH.
>
> Cello: with a bow, explore the v sound as in va va voom.
>
> Snare drum: explore the t sound as in tttt/ttt.
>
> Stringed double base: explore through plucking, the z sound as in zee zee.
>
> Timpani drum: (explore at least four drums) the d sound as in da da da do.
>
> Trombone: explore the r sound as in roo roo row ra.
>
> French horn: (curly one) explore the y sound as in yeah yeah yeah.
>
> Flute: explore the W sound such as in whoo whoo.
>
> Oboe: explore the ng sound such as si<u>ng</u>.
>
> Saxophone: explore the /l/ sound with the tongue held high and slow.

Clarinet: explore with a voiced th sound such as <u>th</u>ese followed by a vowel tha/ the/ tho/.

Violin: explore with a n sound as in no no no.

Viola: (slightly bigger) explore with an m sound as in mum moo.

Exercise 14: Imaginary orchestra, in pairs

Collaborate with a partner and decide on an instrument each to 'play'. Without discussion, create some music from the following genres and begin to play, creating a sound of listening and responding.

Jazz

Pop

Rock

Musical theatre

Opera

Hip hop

Tips for teachers

Taking this exercise further, you could split your cohort into two groups. Your students can change metaphorical instruments for each new piece of music. Ask your students to create a new piece of music for a film score such as a horror movie, or a classical piece of music. You can create a range of genres or musical suggestions with this exercise. Furthermore, you could also bring in listening and responding exercises such as how you would dance to a piece of music created by one group playing their imaginary instruments, whilst the other group must dance to what has been offered. This brings in elements of improvisation, listening, observing and responding to the circumstance which is key to Meisner's work.

Calls and shouts

Understand it

Having worked with the imaginary orchestra, I have found that it helps with listening and responding.

This draws on the work of Arthur Lessac that we touched upon in calls and shouts in Chapter 3. He was a renowned voice and singing coach who founded the concept of the imaginary consonant orchestra. This and Sandford Meisner's repetitive and listening nature in acting techniques, are distinct yet both influential approaches in voice and actor training. Arthur Lessac introduced the consonant orchestra to explore vocal expression. This metaphorical orchestra encompasses the interplay of consonant sounds, emphasising the role in listening and communication of resonance and power. These imaginary instruments serve as a unique framework for vocal exploration. By dissecting the nuance of the consonants and giving each instrument a particular sound offers a rich palette to convey emotion, intention and vibrancy. The consonants play a vital role in creating an impactful vocal and warm-up that supports listening and communication.

On the other hand, the work of Sanford Meisner, as we have acknowledged, emphasises repetition in actor training, revolving around the other scene partner by engaging in repetitive exercises, to cultivate listening, spontaneity, emotional responsiveness and truthful reactions. Both approaches aim to strip away artificiality and encourage actors to live truthfully under imaginary circumstances.

Suggested reading

Maya Angelou, *When Great Trees Fall* (1990), Virago Publishers, US.
William Butler Yeats, *Byzantium. The Collected Works* (2013), New York: Scribner Publishers.

Emily Dickinson, *A Route of Evanescence. The Complete Poems* (2016), Faber & Faber UK.

Further reading

Lessac, A. (1967), *The Use and Training of the Human Voice*, California: Mayfield Publishing Company.
Meisner, S. and Longwell, D. (1987), *Sandford Meisner on Acting*, London: Vintage Original.
Mosely, N. (2014), *Meisner in Practice*, London: Nick Hern Books.
Shakespeare, William (1995), *The Sonnets and A Lovers Complaint*, London: Penguin Classics UK.
Shakespeare, William (2010), *The Complete Works of Shakespeare*, The Arden Shakespeare, London: Bloomsbury.
Sparks, R. (2022), *Meisner and Mindfulness: Authentic and truthful solutions for the challenges of modern acting*, Oxford: Routledge.

7 The Embodied Actor – Konstantin Stanislavski

> When an actor is completely absorbed by some profound moving objective so that he throws his whole being passionately into its execution, he reaches a state we call inspiration. *KONSTANTIN STANISLAVSKI*

> The degree of freedom from unwanted thoughts, and the degree of concentration on a single thought, are the measures, the gauge to spiritual progress. *RAMANA MAHARSHI*

Embody meaning:

1. Tangible, visible forms to ideas or feelings.
2. To represent a quality.
3. Give an expression of spirit.

Introduction

This final chapter epitomises the value and respect that many other acting methodologies sprang from, or in some way connect to, through the pivotal figure of Konstantin Stanislavski.

Stan the Man, or the Godfather as I often refer to him, recognised that the interconnectedness of voice, acting, movement, singing and dance have a respect for authenticity and truth. You will see how the other approaches to acting and movement in many ways refer to his work, either directly or indirectly. I hope that you will see a joined-up approach to voice training and Stanislavski's acting methodology for actor training and development and find the connection through all the other practitioners mentioned in this book. I have concentrated this chapter on a few well-known exercises of Stanislavski, to explore voice, breath, pitch, pace and intention.

Konstantin Stanislavski was the most influential theatre practitioner, having an impact and influence from Russia to the United States and Europe, which impacted a wide range of practitioners that still practice his methodology today. Stanislavski was born in Moscow, and after *conservatoire* training he became known as a great character actor, although he is most famous for his method of actor training. Stanislavski was to later influence a great many acting practitioners such as Uta Hagen, Michael Chekhov, Lee Strasberg and Sandford Meisner, referred to in previous chapters.

Prepare the body – warm-up

Feel the work

Exercise 1: Preparing the body through tension and release

Lie down on the floor on your back, with your eyes closed and your legs out in front of you, with your arms by your side (supine).

Tense up your toes for 3 seconds then release the breath and say AH.

Tense up your legs, squeezing them together, hold them for 3 seconds then release them and say AH.

Tense up your hands into fists. Hold them for 3 seconds then release them and say AH.

Tense up your arms and hands and hold them for 3 seconds then release them and say the sound AH.

Tense up shoulders and hold them for 3 seconds then release them and say the sound AH.

Scrunch up your face and hold for 3 seconds, then release the face and say the sound AH.

Finally, tense up the whole body for 5 seconds, hold and release. And say the sound AH.

Exercise 2: Warm up the senses using the imagination

Sit on a chair or remain lying down with your eyes closed.

Now imagine you are outside sitting on a chair, and it is a sunny day. Notice the air around you, and the smells in the air. Breathe in through the nose and release out through the mouth on a sigh. *How does the air feel?*

You may notice the sun is warm on your face. Notice how your body feels through your visualisation.

Now imagine the weather is changing, and it begins to drizzle lightly with rain and a raindrop falls on your lips. Notice the taste of the raindrop, notice the clouds.

Next, imagine you are walking through the grass on a wet sunny, rainy day.

Explore your senses as you walk through the rain.

Imagine this walk takes you 1 minute. Notice your breath, notice how you walk.

Open your eyes and stand in neutral posture to centre the body. Make connection to the floor, and repeat the exercise of scanning the body, to release tension in a standing pose from head to toe. This can be a daily practice to talk yourself through.

Exercise 3: Quick body scan

Stand in neutral posture and imagine you are noticing each part of your body relax.

Toes: scrunch up, then let the toes relax, breathe in, and breathe out. Imagine you are saying, 'Toes, release, allow, let go.'

Legs: scrunch up, then let the legs relax, breathe in, and breathe out. Imagine you are saying, 'Legs, release, allow, let go.'

Thighs: scrunch up, then let the thighs relax, breathe in, and breathe out. Imagine you are saying, 'Thighs, release, allow, let go.'

Buttocks: scrunch up, then let the buttocks relax, breathe in, and breathe out. Imagine you are saying, 'Buttocks, release, allow, let go.'

Stomach: scrunch up, then let the stomach relax, breathe in, and breathe out. Imagine you are saying, 'Stomach, release, allow, let go.'

Chest: scrunch up, then let the chest relax, breathe in, and breathe out. Imagine you are saying, 'Chest, release, allow, let go.'

Shoulders: scrunch up, then let the shoulders relax, breathe in, and breathe out. Imagine you are saying, 'Shoulders, release, allow, let go.'

Arms: scrunch up, then let the arms relax, breathe in, and breathe out. Imagine you are saying, 'Arms, release, allow, let go.'

Hands: scrunch up, then let the hands relax, breathe in, and breathe out. Imagine you are saying, 'Hands, release, allow, let go.'

Neck: scrunch up, then let the neck relax, breathe in, and breathe out. Imagine you are saying, 'Neck, release, allow, let go.'

Face: scrunch up, then relax the face, breathe in, and breathe out. Imagine you are saying, 'Face, release, allow, let go.'

Breath, sound and imagination

Understand the work

To give powerful moment to authentic, natural and spontaneous performances that captivate an audience, allowing the voice to be free, it is believed through the acting method of Stanislavski that three fundamental things must be in place. Relaxation, concentration and imagination. Relaxation is the foundation upon which rest the 'house of method for actor training'. Without this foundation in place the tension becomes an obstacle for the actor. Acknowledging how the mind and the body talk to each other, where tension can take hold, allows the actor to recognise that tension and the need to release it before work can begin.

Exercise 4: Physical warm-up

Now stand with your legs slightly wider apart and imagine you are punching someone or something, with your left hand across your body on the right side of you. Release a sound of breath on an /f/ on each punch. Punch 5 times across the right side.

Now repeat on the other side, releasing the /f/ through breath on each punch. Punch 5 times across the left side.

Next punch up to the ceiling, releasing the /f/ through breath on each punch. Punch up 5 times.

Now punch down to the floor, releasing the /f/ through breath on each punch. Punch 5 times down.

Finally, repeat the same exercise, adopting the HA sound on each punch.

This is to wake up the back and arms and create simple breath and body sequence.

Exercise 5: Circling body parts releasing the /s/ sustained sound

Standing on one leg, circle the ankle clockwise and anticlockwise 4 times, releasing on the sustained /s/.

Repeat the exercise on the other leg.

Then circle the knees clockwise and anticlockwise 4 times, releasing on the sustained /s/.

Then circle the hips both clockwise and anticlockwise 4 times, and release on the sustained /sh/.

Next circle the shoulders forwards and backwards 4 times, and release on a sustained /s/.

Then circle the arms both forwards and backwards 4 times, and release on the sustained /f/.

Now circle the hands both clockwise and anticlockwise 4 times each way, and release on a sustained SH.

Now drop your chin to your chest, and circle the neck in semi-circles, from shoulder to shoulder, 4 times each way with the nose moving from shoulder to shoulder, and release on a sustained /f/.

Now circle the nose clockwise and anticlockwise 4 times, and release on a sustained /s/.

Finally, circle the eyes 4 times clockwise and anticlockwise and release on a sustained /s/.

Circles of attention and concentration

Exercise 6: Three circles of attention and concentration (video)

Stage 1. The hum

Standing in a neutral posture, relax the jaw by keeping the jaw open but the lips gently closed. Place one palm on your chest and begin humming, creating what you believe is sound coming from your body and back to you.

Next, keeping your hand on your chest as you start to hum, take your hand out at arm's length, still humming, keeping the jaw relaxed and the lips gently closed.

Finally place both your hands on your chest and take them out as if sharing your humming sound to the wider world.

Stage 2. The hum to sound

Now place your hand on your chest, keep it there and begin humming to yourself, then open your oral cavity to a sustained

Figure 7.1 Three circles of attention and concentration.

AH vowel. Imagine you are talking to yourself, a soliloquy (internal).

Next place your hand on your chest and hum, then as your hand moves out to arm's length allow the sound AH to escape. Imagine you are talking to one or two people as a monologue (external).

Finally, take both your hands to your chest and hum, allowing both hands to reach out beyond arm's length, and vocalise the sustained AH sound. Imagine you are talking to the entire world (external plus).

Stage 3. Sound to speech.

Exercise 7: Repeat the circles of attention

Place your hand on your chest and acknowledge 'the self', with a sustained sound of EE, and then intone the word ME.

Place your hand on your chest and acknowledge the other person, at 'arm's length', with a sustained sound of OO, and then intone the word YOU.

Now place both hands on your chest and acknowledge the 'to the world' with a sustained sound of AYE, and then intone the word THEY.

Repeat the exercise again, this time slapping your chest to recall whether you are in the first circle of attention, and self; in the second circle of attention, at arm's length; or in the third circle of attention, and the world.

Practice the work

Now you can take the exercise further by looking at some text listed. Remind yourself of the following: the self, arm's length and out to the world. Notice the different sensations between each physical action. Observe how it affects the text, the breath, the volume and power in each line.

> *Hamlet*, Act 3 Scene 1.
>
> To be, or not to be, that is the question:
> Whether 'tis nobler in the mind to suffer
> The slings and arrows of outrageous fortune,
> Or to take arms against a sea of troubles
> And by opposing end them. To die – to sleep,
> No more: and by a sleep to say we end
> The heartache and the thousand natural shocks
> That flesh is heir to.

How often are you in the first circle – of self?
How often are you in the second circle – of arm's length?
How often are you in the third circle – out to the world?

Exercise 9: Full combo: the self, arm's length, to the world

Next try the sonnet listed and explore all three circles of attention, taking your hands out to the world when you feel it is right.

> Sonnet 23
>
> As an unperfect actor on the stage,
> Who with his fear is put besides his part,
> Or some fierce thing replete with too much rage,
> Whose strength's abundance weakens his own heart;
> So, I, for fear of trust, forget to say
> The perfect ceremony of love's rite,
> And in mine own love's strength seem to decay,
> O'ercharg'd with burden of mine own love's might.
> O let my books be then the eloquence
> And dumb presagers of my speaking breast,
> Who plead for love and look for recompense
> More than that tongue that more hath more express'd.
> O, learn to read what silent love hath writ:
> To hear with eyes belongs to love's fine wit.

Practice the work

Exercise 10: Circles of attention, solo or in pairs

Take an object that is fairly close to you in your hands and look at it for 30 seconds, absorb every detail, every facet, every bit of that object. All the while humming.

Then place it behind your back and recall every detail from memory of the object. You can do this many times to gain greater levels of concentration and how your memory reminds you of every detail.

If you do not have a partner, you can record yourself on your phone and then play back your recollection as you look at the object.

Now imagine a small circle around yourself about a metre all the way around you, and observe every detail within that metre circle only, humming at all times.

Do not be forced to look outside the circle of concentration – just this metre wide and notice everything in 30 seconds, all the while humming. See every detail within that circle.

Now with your eyes closed recall every detail you remember to a partner or onto your phone to record. Play it back.

What did you miss, was your concentration interrupted?

Next take a medium circle about the size of the room you are in. Within 30 seconds see in detail as much as possible. Look at every object, door, cupboard, books, etc. in relation to you, all the while humming, and allow the volume of the hum to be affected.

Closing your eyes recall every detail.

Finally, the large circle of concentration asks you to look as far as the eye can see within your vision. Is there a window? What do you see outside? In 30 seconds recall as much detail as possible whilst humming, and allow the volume of the hum to be affected. With your eyes closed, recall as much detail as possible back on your phone, or to your partner. This large circle of concentration is the most difficult as there are outside influences that can cause us to break our concentration, such as the weather, someone walking past, the trees moving, a dog playing.

Understand the work

The concept of the circles of attention is simple. However, the act of 'doing it' is more complicated and it takes time to develop those skills. Stanislavski believed that actors can be easily affected by the audience and consequently there becomes a need to perform instead of being 'in the moment'. He also believed that an actor's relationship to things on stage are compromised by the magnetic pull of the audience, so he developed a system of using circles of attention and concentration, like drills to be done daily as a warm-up, drilling the circles to create true focus.

Practice the work
Exercise 11: Time sensitive, in pairs

In pairs, move about the space to create a new set of circumstances, using the same exercises, to work on developing circles of attention, as before, only the time limit has decreased to 20 seconds and see what you can recall.

Change the space you are in or move.

Now explore the same exercise with even less time, in 10 seconds. This is less about what you remember but how much you really absorb in the moment, including your breathing and heart rate.

Notice if the reduced time affects what you have remembered.

Does it place pressure on the details you have to recall?

Does it effect the breathing or your heart rate?

Notice if the less time you have to remember the details creates tension in your body.

Is the tension useful?

Practice the work: Full combo

Now that you are aware of the relationship of each of the circles of attention use a speech that you know very well and speak the text from a place of self (first circle), arm's length (second circle) and finally the world (third circle). Notice the physical and vocal energy required for each of these states. Your partner will watch and feedback to you and vice versa. You should be looking out for when there is a change in volume or clarity of the three circles. It may be that only circles one and two are easily identifiable.

Play with the lines of the monologue below, suggesting changes between first circle, to second circle, then to third circle and back. Try this several times over and observe the variation in the circles and the speech. Notice if this affects volume, pace, pitch, resonance and breath.

Try to work on all three stages of the circles of attention and notice if one of the circles is more important than the others. Notice if the volume from self to arm's length, or out to the world, changes. Keep changing the circles to see what works for you.

Play: *Julius Caesar*

Act 3 Scene 2

Friends, Romans, countrymen, lend me your ears;
I come to bury Caesar, not to praise him.
The evil that men do lives after them;
The good is oft interred with their bones;
So let it be with Caesar. The noble Brutus
Hath told you Caesar was ambitious:
if it were so, it was a grievous fault,
And grievously hath Caesar answered it.
Here, under leave of Brutus and the rest –
for Brutus is an honourable mane:
So are they all, all honourable men –
Come I to speak in Caesar's funeral.
He was my friend, faithful and just to me:
But Brutus says he was ambitious;
And Brutus is an honourable man.
He hath brought many captives home to Rome
Whose ransoms did the general coffers fill:

Did this in Caesar seem ambitious?
When that the poor have cried, Caesar hath wept:
Ambition should be made of sterner stuff:
Yet Brutus says he was ambitious;
And Brutus is an honourable man.

Tips for teachers
Using the game Jenga, I sometimes employ this exercise in class. It is helpful for the students to have duologues prepared where they may try the concentration exercise using the game Jenga. The idea is to play the Jenga game, keeping focus on winning the game. Notice the tension between the scene partners. Allow the students to observe the breath, or notice the pace, the tempo, the pitch, the breath and levels of concentration. Are they holding their breath as if this game is an external factor to the scene?

Now try and work the scene again without the game.
How has it helped with concentration, and tension?

Emotional recall

Exercise 14: Emotional memory or emotional recall

Use some rehearsed text that you already know to work on this section.

First, imagine you are smelling some fruit, some coffee, or something else that you enjoy smelling. *What does it remind you of? How does it make <u>you</u> feel? And how does it affect the <u>character</u> feel?*

Speak your text and notice if it affect your heartbeat, the pace, the thought process, the breath or the pitch and tone of words.

Now imagine you are tasting something for the first time. Eat something and really notice how it tastes. *As you bite into it do* you or relish eating it slowly or are you hungry and want to eat it all in one go? Notice how it affects the heartbeat, the pace, the thought process, the breath or the pitch and tone of words

Next, imagine you are hearing something for the first time, something really happy. *How does it make you feel?* Notice how it makes the character feel. Notice how it affects the heartbeat, the pace, the thought process, the breath or the pitch and tone of words.

Now imagine you are hearing something really sad. Notice how it makes you feel, and how it makes the character feel. Notice how it affects the heartbeat, the pace, the thought process, the breath or the pitch and tone of words.

Understand the work: Emotional memory or emotional recall

Stanislavski suggested that you do not interpret your own story, but that you use your imagination to inhabit a character. If you have to play someone who is in fear of their life, he would not suggest that you recreate a fearful moment of your own, but that you analyse the moment, such as your breathing, dark night, warm day. You should not be playing a scene to work on your own anxieties.

Methods of physical action

Exercise 15: Method of physical actions

Imagine you are doing a simple action such as chopping vegetables for dinner. This is a simple physical action, and release a breath.

Now repeat the same physical action and release a sound such as AH.

Next, repeat the same physical action and release a word.

Now imagine you are a chopping those same vegetables and about to tell your child for the first time that they were adopted, and release a breath.

Next repeat the same physical action, release a sound such as OH.

Finally, using the same physical action, release the text you intend to say.

This is how the physical actions affect the emotions.

Exercise 16: Psycho-physical, in pairs

Using your duologues, this exercise explores the relationship between mind and body, where a physical action can create intention by doing something. Therefore, start your scene by doing something, in order to make an impact on your scene partner.

Suggestion 1

Get a glass of water and sip the water every now and again whilst playing your scene and talking to your partner. Continue to drink the glass of water and move away from your scene partner.

What do they notice about you or the scene? How does it affect the breath, the pitch, the pace of the scene?

(Discuss how this drives the scene.)

Continue with a more obvious physical action (which is something we do to further have an impact on our scene partner), the physical activity drives the intention.

Suggestion 2

Now drink a glass of water and get remarkably close to your scene partner.

What do they notice about you or the scene? How does it affect the breath, the pitch, the pace of the scene?

(Discuss how this drives the scene.)

Suggestion 3

Next fold some items of clothing neatly and carefully as you work your scene with your partner (discuss, how it affects, pace, pitch, breath, spontaneity).

Suggestion 4

Finally, try rehearsing the scene again, but with no care whatsoever in the folding of the clothes. Notice the reaction with your scene partner. Discuss how this drives the intention of the scene (discuss how it affects pace, pitch, breath, spontaneity).

Understand the work

The breath, the pace, the pitch and the energy of the lines is affected by what you do to another person, and by what you receive back. Working your way through scenes using a psycho-physical reality, or an emotional memory, allows you to explore the depths of the character you are investigating through the truth and authenticity of the work.

Body scan cool-down

Exercise 17: Cool-down body scan

After an intense set of exercises, I suggest a cool-down, using a body scan, relaxation, mindfulness as imaginary stimuli and sound.

Lie on the floor in semi supine or supine, alternatively you could sit upright in a chair.

Imagine the colour red, now intone a sustained sound of UH as in cup. The colour can be found in the base of the spine and governs strength, stability and encompasses the first three vertebrae and connects with the colon and bladder. The spoken action for this sound is, 'I am here.'

Now imagine the colour orange and intone a sustained sound of OO, as in spoon. The colour is located just below the navel and governs the creative expression and the centre of our creativity. The spoken action is, 'I feel.'

Next imagine the colour yellow, now intone a sustained sound of OH. The colour is located in the area in the centre of your stomach and governs the digestive system and personal power. The spoken action is, 'I do.'

Next imagine the colour green, now intone a sustained sound of AH. The colour is located in the heart centre and governs heart, lungs and is a source of love and connection. The spoken action is, 'I love.'

Now imagine the colour blue and intone a sustained sound of EYE. The colour located in the throat area and governs neck thyroid, jaw, mouth and tongue. It is our source of verbal communication and the ability to speak your truth. The spoken action is, 'I speak.'

Next imagine the colour purple, now intone a sustained sound of AYE. The sound is located between the eyebrows and is the centre of our intuition, this includes our face, eyes and forehead. The spoken action is, 'I see.'

Finally, imagine the colour white or violet, now intone a sustained sound of i EE. The sound is located at the crown of the head and is the centre of knowledge, enlightenment and our higher selves. The spoken action is, 'I know.'

Understand the work

Stanislavski's actor training delves into the psychological, emotional and sensory awareness of performance, contributing to the holistic and personal development of expression. What you may have not been aware of is that whilst we were cooling down and using our imagination to relax through a mind map of the body, we were also working on what is known as the chakras, which we captured in Chapter 1 where we explored the spine through yin yoga and the chakras.

These are considered wheels of energy, which also correspond with the vagus nerve that runs through your body, starting from the base of the skull and brain that leads around the throat, into the heart, down into the diaphragm and through the pelvis. This helps control our emotional wellbeing, autonomic nervous response and affects breath for stress. This is a perfect example of physical work and concentration, imagination and practices combined with scientific anatomy.

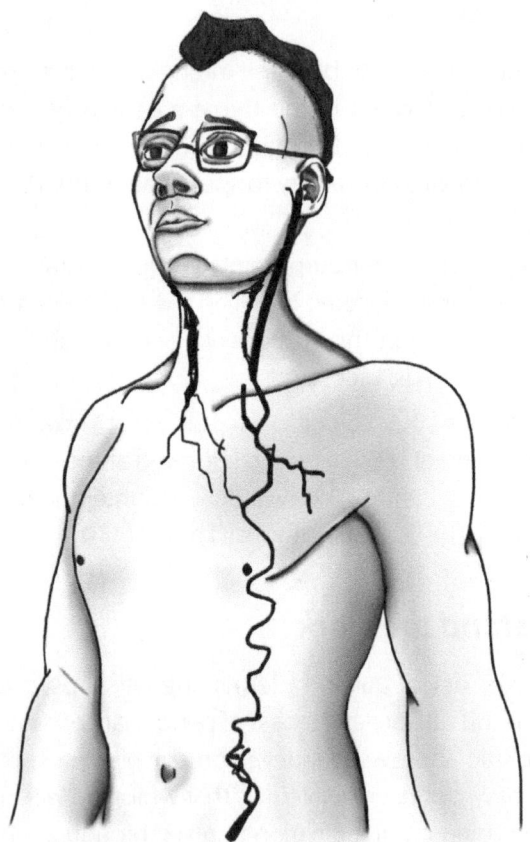

Figure 7.2 The vagus nerve.

Figure 7.3 The chakras.

What are chakras? The chakra is a Sanskrit word meaning wheel or disk. In yoga and meditation it refers to wheels of energy or centres of energy throughout the body.

There are seven main chakras that we have worked through starting at the base of the spine up through to the crown of your head. You can imagine the chakras as swirling wheels of light and energy, the life force, full of vibrancy.

Each chakra can connect with the physical, emotional and psychological states. Working through vibrations and adding sound to our chakras means they are balanced and well placed, open and aligned.

By sounding through the chakras you are restoring balance and being present, in mind and body, experiencing the natural and spontaneous energy that, as Stanislavski expressed, will hold an audience, keeping the voice free through relaxation, concentration and imagination.

The human experience is intricately woven with various dimensions, and Stanislavski, Michael Chekhov, Tadashi Suzuki, Sandford Meisner, Mary Overlie and Rudolph Laban, understood this. These dimensions often involved exploring the interconnectedness of different knowledge centres within the body. The prominent areas are the heart, the head, the gut and the groin, which are often recognised as key centres, influencing emotions, intellect, intuition and instinct.

They all connected with their primary physical being, delving into what makes us tick, and how to develop key ideas to support actor training. As a consequence, we all show through our various skills how to associate feelings, movements and ideas of text through this shared language of how to train actors.

Voice, movement and acting practitioners recognise that the heart centre is often associated with emotions and compassion, which goes beyond the physical organ. 'My heart is breaking.' It is the seat of love, empathy and connection. When decisions are made from the heart, they are driven by a sense of kindness and understanding, cultivating emotional intelligence and fostering meaningful relationships which are essential aspects of harnessing the potential of the heart centre.

The head centre, or the reasoning centre, is the domain of intellect and rational thinking. It encompasses logical reasoning, analysis and problem-solving. When decisions are made from the head, they are often guided by facts, data and critical thinking. Developing cognitive skills and a thirst for knowledge are crucial for tapping into the vast capabilities of the head centre.

The gut centre, the intuition centre; 'I feel it in my gut.' The gut centre is often referred to as the second brain and is associated with intuition and instinct. It is the source of 'gut feelings' and an innate understanding of situations. Trusting your gut involves listening to the subtle cues your body provides, leading to swift and often accurate decision-making. Nurturing this centre involves cultivating mindfulness and being attuned to your inner instincts.

The groin centre drives ambition, passion, purpose, power and creativity. This is often overlooked and is closely tied to physical and instinctual responses. It is associated with survival instincts, sexuality, and the primal aspects of human nature. Balancing the groin centre involves acknowledging and understanding our basic needs and desires, finding harmony between instinctual responses and rational decision-making.

These four knowledge centres are not isolated entities but are interconnected, influencing one another in complex ways.

The complexity of human experience, the heart, head, gut and groin serve as dynamic knowledge centres, each contributing unique qualities to our perception and decision-making processes as actors and beyond. This is the embodied actor, and to recognise and nurture these centres can lead to a more harmonious and integrated approach to navigating the complexities of the choices you make as an actor.

Finally, the exercises and vocal techniques in the Stanislavski system are designed to develop an actor's physical and vocal body, enabling them to deliver authentic, powerful performances by integrating relaxation, concentration, imagination and physical actions. Stanislavski's approach equips actors with the tools they need to fully inhabit their characters and connect with their audience through truth and emotional depth. Whilst Stanislavski created the modern method of acting, one that changed the nature of actor training since the late nineteenth century, many other practitioners were and are influenced by him, or by others who were influenced by him, either directly or indirectly. However, it should not matter what philosophy you prescribe to, only that it supports you, the embodied performer or tutor, and allows you to be creative, imaginative, transformative and flexible in mind and body.

Suggested texts

Walt Whitman, *Song of Myself* (2015), London: Vintage Classics.
Elizabeth Barrett Browning, *How do I love thee*, (1996), Phoenix UK.
William Butler Yeats, *When you are old*, (2015), London: Penguin Classics.
Carol Ann Duffy, *Valentine*, (1995), London: Puffin.
Maya Angelou, *And still, I rise* (1986), London: Virago Press.
T.S Eliot, *The waste land* (2002), Faber & Faber UK.
Paul Laurence Dunbar, *We wear the mask* (2010), Ohio: Kent State University Press.

Further reading

Berry, C. (2000), *Voice and the Actor*, London: Virgin.
Carey, D. and Carey Clark, R. (2010), *Verbal Arts workbook*, London: Methuen.
Donnellan, D. (2002), *The Actor and the Target*, London: Nick Hern Books.
Gutekunst, C. and Gillet, J. (2014), *Voice into Acting, Integrating Voice and the Stanislavski Approach*, London: Methuen Drama UK.
Hanh, Thich N. (1999), *The Miracle of Mindfulness: An introduction to the Practice of Meditation*, Boston, MA: Beacon Press.
Merlin, Bella (2009), *The Complete Stanislavsky Toolkit*, London: Nick Hern Books.
Shakespeare, William (1995), *The Sonnets and A Lovers Complaint*, London: Penguin Classics.
Shakespeare, William (2010), *The Complete Works of Shakespeare*, The Arden Shakespeare, London: Bloomsbury.
Stanislavski, C. (2013), *An Actor Prepares* (Bloomsbury revelations), London.
Stanislavski, C. (2013), *Creating a Role* (Bloomsbury revelations), London.

Appendix 1: Sample curriculum

This voice curriculum sets out to indicate how you may incorporate this workbook into your classes alongside any other acting work the students may do. It may offer more interconnectedness between acting, moving and voice departments within your institution.

These classes have been designed with semesters in mind but can easily move towards a term. This workbook follows a pattern of voice training into each acting or movement skill. I have designed the curriculum based on how I teach voice. However, your students may or may not have come into contact with other practices or methodologies of movement and acting just yet, or may have been exposed to them, therefore this offers the opportunity to embrace the connections with other disciplines.

I have created two semesters, or terms, of a curriculum. The first 'The fundamentals and the foundations', sets out Chapters 1–3 and focuses on posture, breath, yin yoga and tai chi, the acting methods of Michael Chekhov and the stamina work of Tadashi Suzuki.

The second semester, or terms 2 and 3, covers Chapters 4–7 and is entitled 'The advanced interconnectedness of voice, acting and movement', I consider this voice training leading into more in-depth movement of pitch and tune through 'Viewpoints' of Laban and articulation and resonance using the Meisner method. Finally, the last chapter supports the integrated performer through the work of Stanislavski.

Semester 1: The fundamentals and the foundations

The interconnectedness of voice, acting and movement, Chapters 1–3

Week 1: Warm-up in Chapter 1, followed by posture and spine work, plus video.

Week 2: Warm-up in Chapter 1, followed by yin yoga, breath and sound, plus video.

Week 3: Warm-up in Chapter 2, followed by tai chi sequence and breath, plus video.

Week 4: Warm-up in Chapter 2, followed by tai chi sequence and sound, plus video.

Week 5: Warm-up in Chapter 2, followed by tai chi and gestures Michael Chekhov, plus video.

Week 6: Warm-up in Chapter 2, followed by gestures and sound Michael Chekhov, plus, video.

Week 7: Warm-up in Chapter 2, followed by tai chi and Michael Chekhov gestures, plus video.

Week 8: Warm-up in Chapter 3, followed by breath and ten Suzuki walks, plus video.

Week 9: Warm-up in Chapter 3, followed by breath and sound, ten walks, plus video.

Week 10: Warm-up in Chapter 3, followed by breath and sound in standing and sitting statues, plus video.

Week 11: Warm-up in Chapters 1–3 followed by breath and sound in standing and sitting statues, plus video.

Week 12: Review the work and ask students to create their own warm-up of 30 minutes of the work to watch the following week, using any of the exercises you have shown.

Week 13: Watch the warm-ups for precision, rigour and technique.

Week 14: Review the semesters work and allow students to feedback their thoughts in the work. What was challenging for them? What have they taken from the work? This is also a time to correct any misconceptions about the work or common mistakes.

Semester 2: The advanced interconnectedness of voice, acting and movement

Chapters 4–7

Week 1: Warm-up through pitch and pace and 'Viewpoints' in Chapter 4, plus video.

Week 2: Warm-up continues through pitch and pace and 'Viewpoints' in Chapter 4, plus video.

Week 3: Warm-up, pitch and pace continued and further 'Viewpoints' in Chapter 4, plus video.

Week 4: Warm-up through Laban Efforts and articulation in Chapter 5, plus video.

Week 5: Warm-up and continue through Laban Efforts and articulation.

Week 6: Warm-up through resonance and Meisner repetition, Chapter 6.

Week 7: Warm-up to continue with resonance in Chapter 6, plus video.

Week 8: Warm-up continues with resonance in Chapter 6.

Week 9: Warm-up through body scan in Chapter 7, plus video.

Week 10: Warm-up, physical actions and voice in Chapter 7, plus video.

Week 11: Warm-up in Chapter 7 and back to basics.

Week 12: Suggest a 50-minute warm up on all chapters, covering the following: body 10 minutes, breath 10 minutes, resonance 10 minutes, pitch 10 minutes and articulation 10 minutes.

Week 13: Watch the warm-ups and give feedback.

Week 14: Review the work.

An alternative curriculum of two semesters would be to take your students through all the chapters in Semester 1 and then revisit it all on a deeper level in Semester 2.

Appendix 2: Bibliography and resources

Allain, P. (2009), *The Theatre Practice of Tadashi Suzuki*, London: Methuen Drama.
Bain, K. (2015), *The principles of Movement*, London: Oberon Books.
Bainbridge, C. B. (1994), *Sensing, Feelling and Action*, Berkeley, CA: North Atlantic Books.
Bloom, K. and Shreeves, R. (1998), *Moves*, London: Routledge.
Carey, D. and Carey Clark, R. (2010), *The Verbal Arts Workbook*, London: Methuen.
Carnicke, S. M. (2013), *Checking Out Chekhov*. London, Methuen Drama.
Carnicke, S. M. (2023), *Dynamic Acting Through Active Analysis*, London: Methuen Drama.
Chekhov, M. (2002), *To the Actor*, London: Routledge.
Gutekunst, Christina and Gillet, J. (2014), *Voice into Acting, Integrating Voice and the Stanislavski Approach*. London: Methuen Drama.
Langer, Ellen J. (2014), *Mindfulness*, Boston, MA: Da Capo Lifelong Books.
Long, R. (2008), *The Key Poses of Yoga*, Baldwinsville, NY: Bandha Yoga Publication.
Merlin, B. (2009), *The Complete Stanislavsky Toolkit*, London: Nick Hern Books.
Morrison, Annie (2022), *A Moment in Speech*, London: Methuen.
Mosely, N. (2014), *Meisner in Practice*, London: Nick Hern Books.
Newlove, J. (1993), *Laban for Actors and Dancers*, London: Nick Hern Books.
Nicholls, C. (2008), *Body, Breath and Being: A new guide to the Alexander Technique*, Hove: D and B Publishers.
Oida, Yoshi and Marshall, Lorna (1997), *The Invisible Actor*, London: Methuen.

Rodgers, J. ed. (2002), *The Complete Voice and Speech Workout*, Montclair, NJ: Applause.
Rodenburg, P. (1997), *The Actor Speaks*, London: Methuen Drama.
Rushe, Sinead (2019), *Michael Chekhov's Acting Technique, A Practitioner's Guide*, London: Methuen Drama.
Shakespeare, William (1995), *The Sonnets and A Lovers Complaint*. London: Penguin Classics.
Shakespeare, William (2010), *The Complete Works of Shakespeare*, The Arden Shakespeare, London: Bloomsbury.
Suzuki Tadashi (1993), *The Way of Acting*, New York: Theatre Communications Group.

Recommended websites and organisations

www.Voicecare.org.uk
www.Voiceworkshop.co.uk
www.britishvoiceassocation.org.uk
www.vasta.org
www.taichifoundation.org
yinyoga.com

Index

Note: The letter *f* after an entry indicates a page that includes a figure.

acting 145–6
actors
   challenges xiii, 1
   technique xiii–xiv
Alexander, F. M. 17–18
Alexander Technique 10, 17–21
alignment. *See* posture
articulation 121–44
   body, senses, tongue, ears 122–6
   consonants 127–37
   Laban Efforts of movements, breath, sound and text 137–44
   tension 123
   warm-up articulators 126–7
assessment 7
athletes 73
atmospheres 55

behavioural gestures 111
Berry, Cicely xii–xiii
Blanchett, Cate 150
body scans
   cool-down 32–3, 92–3, 180–6
   meditation 32–3
   quick 167
Bogart, Anne, 96
   'Viewpoints' 3, 95, 96
breath 37–68
   athletes 73

belly 44–6, 49–50
breathing styles 39–44
Chekhov, Michael 38, 54–5
directions 55–61, 63
emotion 47
gestures 55, 61, 64–6, 67–8
heart, head, gut and groin 66–7
imagination 50–2, 54–5, 62
inspired tai chi 38–9, 41–4
muscles and anatomy 44–51
nostril breathing 41
phonation/sound 41–4, 51–4
respiratory rate 46–7
sensations 57, 58, 60, 61, 62–3
sound 41–4, 51–4
squats 80–1
support 38
voice 63
Bruford, Rose xii
buddy system 7

calls and shouts 90, 162
chakras 182–4
characters 106–7
   gestures 111
   tempo 114–15
Chekhov, Michael 1, 37, 184
   acting techniques 3
   breath 38, 54–5
   directions and gestures 3

gestures 65
imagination 54–5
To the Actor 37
chest 47–8
Churchill, Carol
　Top Girls 113
classical training xiii
comedy 114
consonants 127–37
　alveolar fricatives 133–4
　alveolar nasal 135–6
　alveolar plosives 129–30
　bilabial nasal 134–6
　bilabial plosives 127–8
　fricatives 131–2
　imaginary orchestras 162
　velar nasal 136
　velar plosives 130–1
　voiceless dental fricatives 132–3
Cox, Brian 150
Culture is the Body (Suzuki, Tadashi) 72
curricula 4

David, Viola 150
Death of England Trilogy (Dyer, Clint and Williams, Roy) 72
Dench, Judi 150
diaphragm 45f, 47–8
digestion 46, 49
Dyer, Clint and Williams, Roy
　Death of England Trilogy 72
dynamic posture 10

E.T. (Spielberg, Stephen) 149
earthing 74–5
embodied actors 165–86
　knowledge centres 184–5
　preparing the body 166–8
　breath, sound and imagination 168–70
　circles of attention and concentration 170–7
　emotional recall 177–8

physical action, methods of 178–80
body scan cool-down 180–6
emotion 47, 66–7
emotional centres 66–7, 184–5
exercises
　accessing the breath 51–2
　alternate nostril breathing 40–1
　alveolar fricatives 133–4
　alveolar nasal 135–6
　alveolar plosives 129–30
　the archer 42
　archetypal gestures and voice 64–6
　back story and sensations 62–3
　backward direction 57–9
　balance and neutral posture 18–19
　balance, in pairs 79
　balloon breath 49f, 50–1
　beach ball breath 50f, 51
　belly bowl 45–6
　bicycle walk 84
　bilabial nasal 134–6
　bilabial plosives 127–8
　bowtie pose 29f
　breath 365 39–40
　breathing styles 39
　calls, shouts and statues 89–90
　caterpillar pose 77f
　changing the shape 108–9
　circles and wraps 15–16
　circles of attention, solo or in pairs 173–4
　circling body parts, releasing on the /s/ sustained sound 169–70
　cockroach shuffle 86
　cool-down and be present – body scan script 32–3
　cool-down body scan 180–1
　cool-down walking meditation 92–3

crab walk 85
cross stomp 85
the crow 42
dangling pose 78
dangling to standing pose 24–5, 26
deer pose 21–2, 26
downward direction 60–1
eagle arms pose 30f
emotional memory or emotional recall 177–8
fingers in sand 42
five-sided box 146
foot rotations for ankles 75
forward direction and voice 55–7
fricatives 131–2
full combo of directions, sensations and voice 63
full combo of gestures and four centres 67–8
full combo: the self, arm's length, to the world 173
further belly bowl 49–50
gaze up at the moon 42
gesture and sound 109–10
gesture, in pairs 110
gestures 109
glass pyramid 150–2
golf ball swing 42
happy baby pose 76f–7
heart, head, gut and groin 66–7
humming bee breath 41
imaginary orchestra, in pairs 161
imaginary orchestra (the self) 160–1
imagination 50–2
improvising around posture 19–20
in pairs, space 101
in pairs, funnels 154
jaws, ears, neck and scalp 124–5

Kabuki shuffle 86
knee to chest pose 75f–6
Laban Efforts movement, breath, sound and text 140–1
Laban Efforts tongue and text 139
Laban Efforts warm up 138–9
lateral squat 80
left direction 61
lips and tongue 123
listening and responding with text 159–60
low-flying dragon pose 22, 26
low pose statues 86–7
Malasana squat 80
method of physical actions 178–9
mid pose statues 87
moving, in pairs 79
neutral posture and text 31–2
ocean breath 40
oyster shell 148
parallel squat 80
part horse's mane 42
physical articulation 126–7
physical warm-up 169
pidgeon ties 84
plie squat 80
poses and text 27–8
poses and voice 25–6
preparing the body through tension and release 166–7
psycho-physical, in pairs 179–80
psychological gestures 64–5
puppet 20–1
push dragon away 42
quick body scan 167
repeat the circles of attention 171–2
responding with active listening 159
ribcage 51
right direction 61

robotic repetition, in pairs 156–7
robotic repetition, the self 155–6
from robotic repetition to easy repetition 158
rollercoaster 53–4
scalp 124–5
semi-supine and active rest 12
separate the clouds 42
sequence 1 (the three treasures) 41–2
sequence 2 with sound 43–4
shape 105, 108
shape of stock characters 106–7
side kick 84–5
side stomp 85
sight 96
single whip 42
sitting poses on the floor 88–9
smell 97
soft palate 125
solo and space 103
sound 97
space 99–100
space, colours and observation 98–9
space, in pairs 103
sphinx pose 23–4, 26
spinal twist pose 22–3, 26
spread eagle wings 42
squat pose Malasana 78f–9
standing and noticing 13
statues 86–90
stomp 82
stomp and moving 84
stroke horse's back 42
sumo squat on toes 80
supported fish pose 23, 26
suppress the alien 148f, 149–50
Suzuki walks 83–6
taste 97
tempo 112–13
text and space 100–1

thread the needle pose 30–1f
three circles of attention and concentration 170–1f
time sensitive, in pairs 175
tiptoes upper pose statue 87
tippy-toes tiny steps 85
toes 74
tongue, the 125–6
topography 116–17
touch 98
ujjayi breath 40
upward direction and voice 59–60
velar nasal 136
velar plosives 130–1
voice funnel 152f–3
voiceless dental fricatives 132–3
vowels 147–8
warm-up 14–17
warm up the body 122
warm-up the senses 96–7
warm up the senses using the imagination 167–8
wide-legged child's pose 24, 26
wide-legged (sumo) squat 80
wind pose 75f–6
exhalation 45f, 48
expressive gestures 111

feedback 7
feet 74–5
Fogerty, Elsie xii
Freeman, Morgan 150

gestures 3, 65, 109–12, 117, 118–19
  breath 55, 61, 64–6, 67–8
Glengarry Glen Ross (Mamet, David) 113
good posture 10, 11, 43
groin centre 67, 185
Grotowski, Jerzy xiii
gut centre 67, 185

habitual posture 17–18, 21
Hamlet (Shakespeare, William) 172
head centre 66, 184
heart centre 67, 184

imaginary orchestras 160–2
imagination 50–2, 54–5
inhalation 45f, 47–8
integration 3
intoning 26

jaws 123, 126
Jones, James Earl 150
Julius Caesar (Shakespeare, William) 176–7

knowledge centres 66–7, 184–5

La Bruyère, Jean de 122
Laban, Rudolph 1, 121, 184
    Laban Efforts of movements, breath, sound and text 3, 137–44
Landau, Tina 96
    'Viewpoints' 95, 96
Lessac, Arthur 89, 162
lessons 4

Mamet, David
    Glengarry Glen Ross 113
    Speed the plough 113
meditation 1, 92–3
Meisner, Sanford 1, 145–7, 184
    acting methods 3, 145–6, 162
    repetition 158, 162
mindfulness 11, 32–4
mood gestures 112
movement 137–44
Much Ado About Nothing (Shakespeare, William) 113, 159–60
multiskilled performers 2
muscle motor holds 107–8

nasal resonance 136
neutral posture 10, 18–20, 21, 31–2
nostril breathing 41

Overlie, Mary 1, 184
    'Viewpoints' 3, 95–6
overview 4–6

pace. *See* pitch and pace
Paradise (Tempest, Kae) 73
Philoctetes (Sophocles) 73
philosophy 6–7
phonation 52–4
pitch and pace 95–119
    gestures 109–12, 117, 118–19
    senses, the 96–9, 122–3
    shape 95, 105–9, 118–19
    space 95, 99–105, 118–19
    tempo 112–16, 118–19
    topography 116–19
posture 9–34
    Alexander Technique 17–21
    breath 43
    cool-down 32–3
    dynamic 10
    good 10, 11, 43
    habitual 17–18, 21
    improvising around 19–20
    mindfulness 11, 32–4
    neutral 10, 18–20, 21, 31–2
    spine and active rest 11–14
    static 10
    warm-up 14–17
    yin yoga 21–32
Prayer Before Dying, A (Yeats, W. B.) xiii
public/private gestures 112

relaxation 34, 126, 168–9
repetition in 155–6
resonance 26, 145–62
    calls and shouts 162
    famous voices 150

listening and responding
156–61
nasal 136
repetition in 155–6
voice funnels 152–5
ribcage 46f, 48, 51
Richard III (Shakespeare, William)
27–8, 67–8, 90–2, 118–19,
142–3
Rose Bruford College of Speech
and Drama xii
Royal Central School of Speech
and Drama xii
Royal Shakespeare Company
(RSC) xii–xiii
RSC. *See* Royal Shakespeare
Company

sample curriculum 187–90
sensations 55
senses, the 96–9, 122–3
Shakespeare, William
Hamlet 172
Julius Caesar 176–7
Much Ado About Nothing 113,
159–60
Richard III 27–8, 67–8, 90–2,
118–19, 142–3
Sonnet 7 31–2
Sonnet 8 98–9
Sonnet 23 173
Sonnet 27 81
Sonnet 73 157
Sonnet 85 141
shape 95, 105–9, 118–19
shoulders 29–32
shouts 90, 162
skills classes 2
soft palate 122, 131, 136
Sonnet 7 (Shakespeare, William)
31–2
Sonnet 8 (Shakespeare, William)
98–9
Sonnet 23 (Shakespeare, William)
173

Sonnet 27 (Shakespeare, William)
81
Sonnet 73 (Shakespeare, William)
157
Sonnet 85 (Shakespeare, William)
141
Sophocles
Philoctetes 73
sound
breath 41–4, 51–4
inspired tai chi 41–4
yin yoga 25–6
space 95, 99–105, 118–19
spatial awareness 102–4
Speed the plough (Mamet, David)
113
Spielberg, Stephen
E.T. 149
spine 9–11f, 29–32, *see also*
posture
active rest 11–14
squats 78f–81
stamina 71–93
cool-down body scan 92–3
performances 72–3
squats 78f–81
statues 86–92
stomps 82–3
walks 74–5, 83–6, 92–3
warm-up 73–8
Stanislavski, Konstantin 145,
184
actor training 181, 165–6,
168–9, 185–6
circles of attention 174–5
embodied work 1, 3
imagination 178
standing 9, 10, 13–14
Star Trek TV series 124
static posture 10
Stewart, Patrick 150
stock characters 106–7
stomps 82–3
Sunshine Boys, The (Simon,
Neil) 114

supine 12
support 7, 21, 118, *see also*
　　Alexander Technique;
　　yin yoga
　breath 38
　Suzuki exercises 72
　walking 92
Suzuki, Tadashi 1, 71, 184
　Culture is the Body 72
　statues 3, 86–92
　walks 3, 83–6
Suzuki Method 71
Swain, Neil xiv

tai chi 1
　breath 38–9
　breath into sound 41–4
Tempest, Kae
　Paradise 73
tempo 112–16, 118–19
tension 25, 123, 169, 175, 177
Thurburn, Gwynneth xii
tips for teachers
　breath 48–9, 53–4
　checking in 14
　concentration 177
　gestures 112
　habitual pose 21
　imaginary orchestras 161
　injuries 14
　inspired tai chi 44
　jaw relaxation 126
　meditation 34
　pitch and pace 119
　space 105
　statue exercises 88
　stomps 83
　students' word choice 16
　tempo 116

voice funnels 154–5
warm-up articulators 127
To the Actor (Chekhov, Michael) 37
toes 73
tone 95
tongues 139–40
Top Girls (Churchill, Carol) 113
topography 116–19
triple threat performers 2

vagus nerve 182*f*
'Viewpoints' 3, 95–119
　Bogart, Anne 3, 95, 96
　gestures 109–12, 117,
　　118–19
　Landau, Tina 95, 96
　Overlie, Mary 3, 95–6
　shape 95, 105–9, 118–19
　space 95, 99–105, 118–19
　tempo 112–16, 118–19
　topography 116–19
vocal folds 52*f*, 53
voice curriculum 187–90
voice funnels 152–5
vowels 147–8

Wade, Andrew xii
walking 10, 74, 75, 92
　Suzuki walks 3, 83–6

Yeats, W. B.
　Prayer Before Dying, A xiii
yin yoga 9, 25
　chakras 182–4
　poses 21–32
　shavasana 12
　sounds 25–6
　spine 10, 12
yoga 1, *see also* yin yoga